A Pilgrimage through Universities

A
PILGRIMAGE
THROUGH
UNIVERSITIES

Charles E. Odegaard

With a Foreword by
RICHARD L. MCCORMICK
and a Postscript by
KEITH BENSON

UNIVERSITY OF WASHINGTON PRESS

SEATTLE & LONDON

Library of Congress Cataloging-in-Publication Data

Odegaard, Charles E.

A pilgrimage through universities / Charles E. Odegaard ; with a foreword by
Richard L. McCormick and a postscript by Keith Benson.

p.   cm.

Includes index.

ISBN 0-295-97760-4 (alk. paper)

1. Odegaard, Charles E.   2. University of Washington—Presidents—Biography.

3. College administrators—United States—Biography.   I. Title.

LD5752.1.O34   1999

378'.0092—dc21

[b]   99-13655

CIP

Contents

Photographs follow page 54.

Foreword

CHARLES E. ODEGAARD LED THE UNIVERSITY OF WASH-
ington as its president during the years when it became the large,
distinguished, modern university we know today. No matter who
had been at the university's helm between 1958 and 1973, the enrollment would almost certainly have soared and new disciplines would
have been established. Except for Odegaard's leadership, however,
the university's academic profile would not have risen in all the ways
it did. Through his efforts, the University of Washington—which
had formerly been a respectable regional university—now indis-
putably ranks among the nation's top public research universities.

As the chapters on his presidency make clear, Charles Odegaard wanted above all to influence the university's intellectual life.
"I cannot imagine being a president," he writes, "without also being involved in concerns for the particular business of the university—learning and teaching" (p. 163). Odegaard's academic
involvement took countless forms, but perhaps none was more important than inspiring cooperation across the traditional academic
boundaries and bringing into the administration faculty who were

vii

committed to what he calls "joint intellectual ventures and exchanges" (p. 166). In his inaugural address he called upon the university community to bring educational greatness to the western United States. During his time as president that greatness was achieved.

Although the University of Washington has continued to grow and change in the years since Odegaard's presidency, it is striking to recognize the similarities between his challenges and our own today. As enrollment grew, there was a constant tension between the need to provide access for thousands of new students and the demands of maintaining academic excellence. Because state budgets were constrained, sometimes painfully so, there were tough choices to make and never enough dollars to achieve all the university's goals. In that context, it became all the more important to defend and explain a world-class research university within the political environment of the state of Washington—a task that was no easier in Odegaard's time than it is today.

Among his greatest legacies are the increased diversity of the university student body and his humane leadership during the student protests of the late 1960s and early 1970s. Odegaard put in place many of the programs that we still use to maintain and support the diversity upon which the excellence of everyone's education depends. But he also insisted that the university should "stick to its purpose as an educational institution rather than a political instrument" (p. 194). During his day the University of Washington became the finest educational institution in the northwestern United States, and everyone associated with the university remains in his debt.

RICHARD L. MCCORMICK
President, University of Washington

A Prefatory
Comment

AS I BEGIN TO WRITE THIS STORY OF MY LIFE IN MY eighty-fourth year on this globe, I am struck by the fact that I have spent more than sixty of my years in colleges and universities—as undergraduate, graduate student, faculty member, dean, president, and president-emeritus. These academic institutions are complex, sui generis, and often poorly understood. Sometimes they are little appreciated by much of the general public. Sometimes they are even inadequately perceived by the academics within them. The principal story I have to tell, then, is my experience over many years in a continuing association with a succession of academic institutions.

But my story starts with a paradox and a mystery. The paradox is that none of my forebears, with the slight exception of my maternal grandfather whom I shall describe later, had any experience in higher education. This may not have been too unusual for one of my generation, for in 1899–1900 only three percent of Americans aged twenty to twenty-four were enrolled in college. By the time I became a student at Dartmouth College in 1928, only ten percent of Americans of that age group were so enrolled. But, except for four years of service in the Navy during World War II, I have spent my years from seventeen to eighty-four in association with colleges and universities. From that paradox emerges the mystery: What circumstances led me to depart from the path of business entrepreneurship my father and other relatives had chosen, and instead enter Dartmouth College at seventeen in 1928? Once enrolled at Dartmouth, I began an association with academic institutions destined to continue the rest of my life.

A Pilgrimage through Universities

Pre-College
Prelude,
1911–1928

TO EXPLORE THE MYSTERY AND THE PARADOX, LET ME begin at the beginning. I was born Charles Edwin Odegaard on January 10, 1911, in Chicago Heights, Illinois, as the son of Charles Alfred Odegaard and Mary Cord Odegaard. I feel that fate was very kind to me in providing my particular parents. My father was born in Norway on July 1, 1880, but by the time he was about three months old he had reached Chicago in the company of his father, his mother, and his five-year-old brother, Theodore. My paternal grandfather had learned to speak English in Norway and had aspirations to come to the United States. Something of his attitude toward America was revealed many years later when my father described to me a family incident in about 1896 when his older brother, Theodore, had failed to vote in an election shortly after his twenty-first birthday. When my grandfather learned of this action, or rather lack of action, on Theodore's part, he assembled the whole family, which by then included six sons and a daughter. He deplored Theodore's failure to exercise his obligations of citizenship in a democracy and expressed the hope that none of his children would ever in the future be delinquent in their obligations as American citizens.

My grandfather also insisted that English be spoken within his family. The result was that the three oldest brothers (Theodore, Charles, and Ralph) developed little proficiency in Norwegian. The younger children (Julia, Arent, Harry, and Edward) were less exposed to their father's influence because of his early death in about 1897. They were more exposed to their mother's use of Norwegian, and therefore became more fluent in that tongue than their older brothers.

While there were ethnic communities in Chicago when the Odegaards arrived in 1880, the family did not settle in a Scandinavian enclave. Their next-door neighbors, the Bruntons, of Scottish origin, befriended them and introduced at least my father to the Presbyterian Church. The Bruntons' daughter, May, was my father's contemporary, and their friendship endured throughout their lives. I remember her as a gracious Mrs. Reynolds, wife of a top executive of the Armour Company, living near my parents in Glencoe, Illinois, when I was college age.

Ties with Norway faded quickly for my Norwegian grandparents. My grandfather left in Norway only a sister, a school teacher who never married. My grandmother had only a brother, a ship captain who was lost in a sinking, and who had not married. They apparently had little reason to renew contact with anyone abroad. The Odegaards quickly became Americans. The only Norwegian elements I can recall from my youth were various forms of Norwegian cookies for the Christmas season which my father's sister distributed during the holidays.

My paternal grandfather had acquired the skills of a cabinetmaker in Norway, and his particular forte was designing household furniture. At the time of his arrival in Chicago the economy was favorable, and the era of building brownstone mansions was beginning. The leading Chicago furniture store, which catered to the wealthy, instituted a custom-design section, and my grandfather was soon in charge of the design and construction of fine hand-crafted pieces. During the great Chicago World's Fair of 1893, he won a grand prize for designing and crafting a bedroom set. My father remembered seeing his father carving and recarving two doves facing each other which were then mounted on the headboard of the double bed in that set.

By the late 1880s, my grandfather had saved enough capital to join with two other men in a move to Lawrenceberg, Tennessee, just above the Alabama border, where they established a furniture factory that used the hardwoods available locally. Within a few years, my grandfather's furniture factory business crumbled and his savings disappeared. He decided to bring his family back to Chicago, where fortunately he was able to return to his previous post and continue his productive career in design. At the same time, the oldest son, Theodore, revealed his substantial artistic skill in the design of ornamental ironwork for stairway rails, carriage gates, and other ornaments for elegant housing.

This artistic capacity appeared in different forms in three brothers younger than my father. Ralph became the chief designer of men's suits for one of the largest manufacturers. By the mid-1920s, he had established a small factory for the production of the highest quality suits for elegant shops. After a very successful beginning, the Great Depression in the early 1930s destroyed this venture, but Ralph was able to reestablish himself in the 1940s as designer and producer of individually tailored suits for Oviatt's in Los Angeles, a store that catered to the elite in the burgeoning movie industry.

Another brother, Arent, had, I believe, no advanced or formal training in architecture but he did produce a number of apartment buildings in a three-story form common in Chicago. Yet another brother, Edward, became a top sales officer in one of the very big cotton textile corporations that produced household goods such as sheets, pillow slips, bed covers, curtains, tablecloths, and napkins.

I heard him described by others in this business as very design conscious, capable of choosing outstanding designs for fabrics which quickly became popular and widely imitated by other textile mills. At a given moment he would stop all manufacture and initiate a new design, and it would set the next fashion in household textiles.

Despite the obvious design capacity of my paternal grandfather and uncles, I can make no claim to such skills for myself. The best I can do is to appreciate greatly the innovative artistic talents of others who have capacities I sadly lack.

In 1896, the Odegaard family was struck by a double tragedy, the death within a short period, probably from tuberculosis, of both my grandfather and his oldest son, Theodore, who had also been quite successful in business. My father, as the surviving oldest son, had to leave school and seek employment. He began by wrapping packages at Montgomery Ward, attaining a skill which continued to be evident in later years in his wrapping of Christmas packages for gifts to family and friends. By a decade later, he had acquired a growing knowledge about mechanical tools for the making and maintenance of industrial equipment and was working for the Railway Supply Company then located in Chicago Heights, Illinois, the site for the maintenance shops for the engines and cars of a number of major railroads. It was there that he was destined to meet and marry my mother, Mary Cord.

My maternal grandfather's father was born in Lincolnshire, England, where he acquired the skills of a millwright, a builder of mills for grinding grain, often powered in those days by water running in a stream. He came to the United States as a young adult, married an American wife with an extensive British ancestry in this country, and then moved his own family from place to place in Illinois, Wisconsin, Iowa, and Nebraska, where he built flour mills, one after the other. He apparently preferred building mills to participating in milling operations over any length of time in any one place. He had a daughter and several sons, one of whom was my grandfather, Charles Edwin Cord, who was born in 1866. The latter married Susan White, whose family had been in the United States for some generations, and their first child was my mother, Mary Cord, born in 1886. A couple of years later, they had a son who was known to me as Uncle George.

My grandfather's early employment was as a telegrapher and agent in charge of a railroad station. He then developed a rather surprising ambition, to enter medical school though he had no college education. This meant among other things that he had to acquire some background in Latin. My mother remembered that as a small child she would be asked by her mother to walk to the railway station to deliver luncheon to her father, who, during a lull in other activities, would be studying Latin. He was indeed admitted in 1896 to the Rush Medical College in Chicago, and graduated with an M.D. degree in 1900. He entered the practice of medicine in Chicago Heights, and was a much respected physician there until his sudden death in 1924.

As a medical student at Rush, he was required to have his own microscope. I remember a number of instances during my childhood when my mother would leave me with him in his doctor's office. From the drugstore fountain below, he would order a glass of soda water for each of us, and then he would take down his microscope to show me slides. On one summer's day a grasshopper flew in through an open window and I caught it. My grandfather then dissected it and let me see its parts magnified. I remember particularly his identifying the projections on its legs that it used in making sounds. Apart from being named for him, my material inheritance from my grandfather was that microscope, which I have now passed on to my grandson who was named Charles for me.

During my mother's childhood, her parents separated, and for some years she lived with her mother, who became a nurse. As a teenager, my mother attended a finishing school in Springfield, Illinois. Following the death of her mother, she returned to her father's home in Chicago Heights, a two-story wood Victorian house of which I still have a few memories. There was a separate structure that I remember as a garage, but it was first used as a carriage house for a horse and buggies. My grandfather's brother was an early Cadillac dealer and finally convinced him he should buy an automobile. Thanks to his brother's intervention, he acquired a Cadillac touring car that had been featured in the 1911 automobile show in New York.

That car created some stir at the New York show because, instead of being painted black like others, it was gray. I was born in 1911, and I remember being placed in that car in the seat next to my grandfather and feeling a little uneasy because my legs could not reach the floor. Two days after first typing the preceding sentences, I had an astonishing experience. While walking through the parking area between the shopping street and harbor front of Poulsbo, Washington, on September 14, 1991, I saw parked there a beautifully preserved and still operational 1911 Cadillac touring car, but it was painted black! I waited some time, hoping that the owner would appear, but I had to leave this car dating from the year of my birth without meeting the owner.

With my mother living in her father's home in Chicago Heights, and my father working for the Railway Supply Company in Chicago Heights, it was fated that they should meet. They were married in November 1907, when my father was twenty-seven and my mother twenty-one. Their first child was a daughter, who died within her first year. I was born in Chicago Heights on January 10, 1911, and was followed by my sister Marjorie on March 31, 1916.

Early Childhood

DURING 1911, my first year, my father chose to accept a connection with a new business venture in Chicago, the Federal Machinery Sales Company, which had been initiated by an older man experienced in the marketing of machine tools for heavy industry. It was set up to service the needs of a substantial area of the Middle West centered in Chicago. Within a few years, my father became the chief officer as president, a position he retained until declining health led to his retirement in 1942.

This change in my father's employment in 1911, shortly after my birth, necessitated the family's move to Chicago, where my parents rented the upper apartment in a two-story brick building on Winnemac Avenue on the North side, in what I believe is the Edgewater area. An unusual aspect of the otherwise residential character of the neighborhood was the presence a block away of the Essanay studio, one of the early centers for filming movies. It flourished in the earlier half of the second decade of the twentieth century as a location for making movies with such actors as Ben Turpin, Gloria Swanson, the Beery brothers, Wallace and Noah, Charlie Chaplin, and Francis X. Bushman.

Bushman was a special idol of the ladies. That he was a married man with five children was not widely acknowledged at that time. In fact, he lived with his family across the street from our apartment. His son, Francis X. Bushman, Jr., was my age and an admirer and frequent user of my child's vehicle called, I believe, an Irish Mail. That son subsequently had a brief career as a movie actor, and by a curious chance I encountered him in the 1930s at a resort hotel in Wisconsin. I still recall having seen small crowds gathered in public spaces in our Chicago neighborhood to watch the filming of a movie scene produced before the movie industry's early exodus to California.

From the beginning of my life in Chicago in 1911, my father had an automobile, a touring car, but I still remember incidents involving horses. I recall seeing a handsomely dressed Francis X. Bushman riding a white horse (on Sundays?) in the neighborhood. The policeman who patrolled the streets in our area rode a horse and would pick up a youngster and hold him in the saddle for a brief ride. The horse was so beloved by all of us that he was nicknamed Sweet William. On his final day before retirement, the street was lined with mothers and kids to bid him farewell and to give him candies. Another, and a very impressive sight, was that of a team of hefty horses drawing a wagon loaded with kegs of beer. The most appalling sight was seeing the shooting of a horse that had been drawing a milk wagon and had fallen on the icy street, badly breaking a leg. Memory can indeed be a strange repository.

Grammar School

BY 1916, the time for me to enter grammar school, my family moved to a larger apartment in a three-story, six-apartment building at 1231 Farwell Avenue. It had three bedrooms—one each for my parents, my sister, and me—and also a guest room, a maid's room off the kitchen, a dining room, a drawing room, and a so-called sunparlor. This building was half a block west of Sheridan Road, the principal boulevard running north from the city center of Chicago and paralleling the sandy beach of Lake Michigan only a block to the east. This northernmost section of Chicago adjacent to the lake was known as Rogers Park. A scattering of single-family houses on generous lots had been built therein, but three-story apartments like the one occupied by my family had begun to appear. But there were still wooded lots scattered about which gave a parklike impression. I remember seeing the tracks of rabbits in the snow in winter, and in grammar school I won a prize for spotting more kinds of birds than my classmates. It would not take many years in the 1920s for the area to be covered with apartment buildings and to become a home primarily for invading English sparrows.

I began my schooling at the Eugene Field Grammar School, something like six blocks away from home across residential streets which were not heavily traveled. I have few memories of these early grades, but one is easy to recall. A patriotic recapitulation of our nation's early history was developed for presentation in a school assembly. A prepared script describing a succession of historic occasions was read to the audience. On one side of the stage a large picture frame had been erected with a curtain that could be opened at a suitable moment to reveal a scene illustrative of the event described by the speaker. It fell to my lot to be a substitute George Washington. With the help of my mother, I obtained from a costume supplier an eighteenth-century outfit complete with a white wig. At the appropriate moment, I was revealed to the audience in all my finery in a relevant pose. At the conclusion of the assembly we were all dismissed for the day. For some unaccountable reason, I chose to start home still in my costume and carrying my regular clothes. During a bit of horseplay with fellow students shortly after starting on our walk home, I suddenly heard a ripping sound as the seam in the back of my trousers parted. To make matters worse, we schoolboys seemed to encounter an unusual number of adults along the way. I remember my embarrassed efforts, whatever our angle of approach, to face around them as we passed one another!

As I approached the point of entry into the seventh grade, my parents moved the family residence to a similar apartment building on Jonquil Terrace within a block of Sheridan Road to the west and within two blocks of the northern border between Chicago and Evanston. At that time a new school was under construction to accommodate students enrolled in the upper grades of grammar school. However, six portable metal schoolrooms had been positioned beside one another in a cluster on a neighboring block. I was chosen to ring the handbell at the hourly change of classes. This meant that I had to watch my wristwatch so as to slip outdoors just before the change of hour to walk between the buildings while clanging the bell. As the school year opened for my eighth grade in the new Gale School, an electrical system relieved me of the responsibility as bell ringer. In June 1924, I completed a happy experience in grammar school.

Secondary School

IN THE FALL OF 1924, I entered the newest high school, and the northernmost one in Chicago, the Nicholas Senn High School. This school was some distance from my family's apartment near the northern border of Chicago, but fast commuting was fairly easy for me. Our apartment was a few blocks from the northernmost station on the north line of the El, Chicago's inexpensive rapid transit system. The Senn High School was also only a few blocks from an El station, so my trip between home and Senn could be accomplished quickly and cheaply.

Chicago had some technical high schools and some academic high schools. Senn was a good example of the latter. The English teacher in my second year was a demon on grammar who demanded that we get it right. All I ever learned about grammar must have come from her. The English teacher in my third and fourth years was a gentle soul, steeped in English literature and the culture from which it came. She had made numerous trips to England, and enriched our understanding with her comments on the culture reflected in the English poetry and prose we were reading. A history teacher certainly fed my interest in the complexity of stories of past events. And then there was Augusta Stuart, appropriately named by her classical professor father. She was a hard driving, dramatic teacher par excellence of Latin. Her students behind her back referred to her as the "Old Roman." You will hear more about her later.

I am convinced I received a very good academic education at Senn High School. Attention was still very much focused on the educational program itself, but there were some other activities, and they sometimes brought one in contact with the founding principal of the school, Mr. Buck, an impressive but approachable man, who was in office during my four years at Senn. I had some contact with him in connection with various school activities in which I became involved. My major enterprise was associated with a city-wide cleanup of Chicago, in which students of the various high schools organized the drive in their own area of the city. I was the leader of our drive, and Senn received the top award for student service to the area.

I have little memory of much in the way of organized sports or any facilities for large audiences at sports events. I do recall outdoor performances by the large Senn School Band. One of my life-

long friendships was with a classmate, Warren Peterson, a horn
player who enjoyed being in the band. On several occasions during
my days as a high school student, John Philip Sousa conducted the
Senn Band. Such little musical talent as I possessed was confined
unfortunately to the piano, and my level of competence did not involve participation in group activity.

Odegaard Family Life

THROUGHOUT THEIR ADULT LIVES together, my father and
mother lived in the Chicago area until the last several years before
my father's death in 1944, when they owned and lived in a pleasant
small house in Lake Worth, Florida. By those years, I was immersed
in faculty duties at the University of Illinois, and then at sea in
the U.S. Navy with no opportunity to visit them in Florida during
World War II.

Both my father and mother liked many kinds of people and
were attentive to friends. They had a distinct preference for enter-
taining friends at home. My mother could always produce a delicious dinner beautifully served, not infrequently on short notice.
My parents' tendency to entertain guests at home was encouraged
by the presence of a guest room in their apartments and then in
their houses. The resident guest or guests would often be joined by
other local guests. After all the guests had been assembled, my sister and I would enter the living room to be presented and to greet
the guests, and then to withdraw discreetly. It transpired years later
that my wife Betty had grown up in a similar household, and shared
a similar presumption about home being the preferred place to entertain friends.

My father's family, so far as I know, seemed to be devoid of any
strong religious prejudices. Over the years, my father and mother
maintained a loose Presbyterian tie with some church attendance
for them and Sunday school for me and my sister. My mother's cou-
sins included a few somewhat waspish Protestants. Her brother,
however, married a loyal Irish Catholic and later in life became a

convert to Catholicism. It was with that immediate family that my parents and I maintained the closest ties over the years. Among my parents' close friends, there were also two Jewish couples. My father and mother set a model for religious and racial tolerance.

Neither parent had the opportunity for a full high school education or, of course, for any college experience, but they both took a substantial interest in the schooling of their children. They were in regular contact with our schoolteachers and were aware of various school events. As for their own intellectual pursuits, my father maintained a steady interest in general news about current events, and my mother was an avid reader of books, not only recent novels but also literary works of the last century particularly. The family library included a sizable collection of the principal works of well-known authors of the eighteenth to early twentieth centuries, some of which came from my mother's father's library after his death in 1924. As a high school student, I found myself devouring many historical novels which were often at hand in the family collection. I recall a heavy, worn, red-bound French historical novel by Eugene Sue, which I feared I could never finish but which I could not put down until I finally reached the end. I think this family environment must have preconditioned me for history as a discipline.

A significant part of my upbringing was family traveling, often by auto from Illinois to Massachusetts, Connecticut, and New York as well as to Ohio, the sites of machine tool manufacturing plants, where my father could combine business contacts with vacations. In addition, there were purely pleasure trips to Iowa, Wisconsin, Minnesota, and Michigan where, among friends and relatives, a city boy like me could discover different ways of living beside lakes and among fields and forests.

By the time I entered high school, my father had started an interesting habit of asking me (in summer when schools were closed) to ride the El to downtown Chicago and walk several blocks to his office in time to go to luncheon with him and several of his business friends. My function was principally to listen, but from time to time I was fascinated by what I heard. I have never been sure as to my father's intent. It may have been to stir my interest in business, though I do not recall his ever trying openly to steer me toward his business in machine tool distribution.

As I approached the senior year of high school, a major change of family residence occurred. My parents had commissioned an architect to design and supervise the building of a house at the extreme southern border of the residential town of Glencoe, one of the suburbs north of Chicago. It was serviced by an electric railway that connects with the Chicago El system, and which could thus provide me with a relatively fast commute to Senn High School. I decided that I wanted to complete my senior year at Senn and was permitted to do so by my parents and by the school authorities. To my surprise, I ended my years in high school at Senn as co-valedictorian with my classmate, Dorothy Welch.

My Introduction
to Higher Education,
1928–1932

BY THE BEGINNING OF MY SENIOR YEAR IN HIGH
school, a major question before me and my parents was not
whether I would go to college, but where. The answer presumably
was quickly reached. It was Dartmouth College in Hanover, New
Hampshire, which enjoyed the enthusiastic endorsement of one of
my father's oldest friends, Newman Marsilius, the founder of a machine tool manufacturing company in Bridgeport, Connecticut.
On his many business trips to Chicago, he was a guest in our home,
and loud in his praise of Dartmouth and its beautiful New Hampshire setting. He had fallen in love with the area shortly after his
graduation from the Massachusetts Institute of Technology, when
he served as a consultant to a small manufacturing company in
Lebanon, New Hampshire, a town several miles from Hanover and
Dartmouth. Buoyed by his enthusiasm, I had acquired and submitted an early application for admission to the College.

Shortly thereafter, my Latin teacher at Senn, Miss Stuart, told
me about the competitive examinations in various high school
subjects for tuition scholarships offered by the University of Chi-

cágo. She urged me to enter the examination in Latin. Naively, I shunted aside the suggestion with the affirmation that I was going to go to Dartmouth. The thought that I might not be admitted to Dartmouth had not entered my head. Reality caught up with me in time to take the Latin examination at Chicago. I did win a scholarship there, which I declined, because Dartmouth did admit me as a freshman in September 1928.

Concerning my admission to Dartmouth: One day early in my sophomore year, I was walking across the central green of the campus when I saw coming in my direction the College's director of admissions. We students in those days were polite, and I said, "Good morning, Sir." To my surprise, he stopped and addressed my by name: "Odegaard, you have been a great help to me." He then explained that the College had a long history of admitting as freshmen mostly graduates from prep schools in the New England and Middle Atlantic states who had also presented scores on the College Board examinations. In the early 1920s, the College had begun admitting some students from more distant parts of the country, and they were more often graduates of public high schools. He found himself having to defend this new policy to established Dartmouth alumni groups who argued that the College was admitting students whose academic quality was inferior to that of prep school graduates and therefore reducing places for sons of the alumni. I do not know where my grades placed me in rank at the end of my freshman year, but he was using my freshman scores as an example of a well-qualified student from a public high school who had not presented scores from College Board exams.

Collegiate Life at Dartmouth

IN 1928, most freshmen at Dartmouth arrived by train to neighboring White River Junction, Vermont. All were assigned by the College to designated rooms with designated roommates in the dormitories; all freshmen were required to take their meals in a particular hall in the College Commons. In retrospect, I believe that this requirement of year-long common dining for freshmen, typically strangers to the Dartmouth community, helped to forge rather quickly bonds of friendship supplemented also by encounters with upperclassmen in dormitories, recreational activities, and in actual college courses.

As for living quarters, I found myself assigned to a two-room suite in a fairly new dormitory, Gile Hall, which consisted of a bedroom with two cots, two dressers, two straight chairs, a clothes closet, and a study with two desks, two straight chairs, and two reading chairs. Down the hall was a washroom with basins, showers, and toilets. I found that I shared these accommodations with a College-assigned roommate, Morgan Hobart, a Californian whose prior education had been principally in New England prep schools. As a consequence of these associations, he arrived at Dartmouth with a number of ready-made friendships in the freshman class. The two of us managed the common burdens of roommates amicably enough, but we tended to go our separate ways.

As I noted earlier, it was in the early 1920s that Dartmouth began recruiting students on a more national basis. There were still instances of regional and prep-school snobbery. However, it was my experience that once students resided in the isolated but charming Hanover, where there was little beyond the Dartmouth community, the residue of previous associations had little effect on the forging of warm human friendships among the College student population.

I arrived at Dartmouth in September 1928 with only a few prior friends in the student body, but among Gile Hall residents I quickly found new friends. One of them was Charles Ryan from Fall River, Massachusetts. With Ryan I formed a close friendship which was to endure to his death shortly after his retirement as General Attorney of AT&T. I will write more about him later.

I remember one incident in my sophomore year, when four of us who had been freshman residents in Gile Hall agreed at midday to gather at six o'clock that evening in a particular restaurant on Main Street. Three of us appeared at the appointed time, but Bill

Gerstley from Philadelphia had not yet arrived when the three of us decided to take seats in a nook to order dinner. We had finished our soup and just begun the main course when our missing friend arrived. As he approached the table, the waitress asked him what he wished to order. He answered, "A glass of water and a toothpick." From this allusion to a starvation menu, we first learned of the crash of the New York Stock Exchange that day, the prelude to the Great Depression. Bill explained that he had received a telegram that afternoon from his father, telling him to expect an important telephone call at six that evening. Bill had remained in his room for that call. His father informed him that he had bought stock on margin and at the moment was in need of cash to cover his indebtedness. Bill had recently received an inheritance from a relative, and he had cash in his own bank account, and thus was able to come to the rescue. You will have to hear more about the Great Depression later.

Another opportunity for forging new friendships came in the course of our sophomore year, in the fraternity system. Freshmen were not permitted by the College to join fraternities. My memory is that there were perhaps thirty organized Greek fraternity houses on campus. The College imposed a schedule for open house receptions for potential candidates from the sophomore or upper classes, following which election to membership could occur. While the total club membership could be greater, no more than fifteen juniors or seniors could have rooming accommodations in any fraternity house and no meals could be served in them. These regulations permitted contributions to diverse living arrangements for Dartmouth students and at the same time encouraged them to retain a strong loyalty to the College as a whole, a loyalty further encouraged by the relative isolation of the Hanover community.

In the course of my sophomore year, I was elected to Beta Theta Pi and came to know well a Beta classmate from Bayside, Long Island, James B. Moore, a champion skipper of sailboats, a good businessman, and a friend until his death in 1991. Jim and I were able to share in our junior year a first-floor room in the Beta

House just large enough to accommodate our desks, dressers, reading chairs, and a closet. Single beds for each resident student were placed in the attic space on the third floor. The windows of this space were left open year round. Hanover winters quickly taught one to buy heavy pajamas, wool sheets, and the heaviest Hudson's Bay wool blankets. The coldest temperature I experienced in the attic bed space was 40 degrees below zero!

The Beta House in my time at Dartmouth served well the social purposes of the fraternity. Across the back of the building there stretched a sizable room with a high ceiling suitable for parties on those relatively rare occasions when students from Wellesley, Vassar, Smith, et cetera, might be imported to Hanover for special events like the Winter Carnival. Another unusual feature of the Beta House was its substantial library of books, the gift of a loyal alumnus, which often included works referenced in classroom instruction.

The College had a ban on autos for freshmen, but not for the upper classes. I returned as a sophomore to the College from Chicago in 1929 in a used Nash two-seater coupe. One could reduce the automobile mileage in those days by driving from Chicago to Detroit and boarding an overnight steamer-car ferry to Buffalo. A long day's drive the next day might bring one to Hanover that evening.

I arrived in Hanover as a junior in September 1930 in a new Chrysler open roadster. The story behind my acquisition of that car is an instance of my father's behavior that I have previously described. In the early summer of 1930, my family planned another one of a number of visits with good friends in other cities, this time with the Trainor family in Detroit. While there, my father telephoned an old business friend who had previously been a top officer in a large Illinois corporation, but who had left that post to become second man after Walter Chrysler, Sr., in the Chrysler Corporation. My father was invited to lunch at Chrysler headquarters, and I was included in the invitation. Our host quizzed me on my life at College and then began telling me about a newly styled and engined Chrysler roadster. Its radiator, instead of being flat like all other cars, had a V-shaped front. By the time we finished lunch, he had summoned the Chrysler test driver, who gave me the fastest ride I would ever want to have, in a handsome cream and white, new-style V-front car. I do not know what kind of a deal was made, by my father bought one of those cars for me.

In early September 1930, I traveled to Hanover in that new car with my friend from Senn High School days, Warren Peterson. His classes at Lake Forest College in Illinois began later than mine at Dartmouth, so he could return to Illinois from our trip to Hanover in time to begin his college year. As we drove eastward across country in those days, the highway generally traversed the main street of the towns, with major cross streets indicated by stop signs or green-red lights. It became a common experience as we stopped at crossings on innercity streets for pedestrians to quiz Warren and me in our open roadster about our handsome new car.

They sometimes expressed interest in another passenger in the car, my dog Barney, a beautiful and generally well-behaved Irish red setter. In Hanover, it was not uncommon to see a student walking with a dog, and occasionally a dog would accompany its master to class. I do not remember any untoward incidents in classrooms as a result of these canine-human friendships. Jim Moore, who was to be my roommate in our junior year, welcomed Barney to our quarters in the Beta House, and none of the fraternity brothers raised any objections. When left alone during my absences from the house, Barney remained in Jim's and my personal room. At the time we parted for home at the end of our junior year, Jim and I agreed to share the same room again in our senior year.

In September 1931, I arrived in Hanover somewhat later than in the previous year, and as I drove up to the Beta House I saw a number of brothers sitting on the porch. I opened the car door to let Barney out, and he headed for the porch. From somewhere in the crowd a hefty German Shepherd emerged, making a straight line for Barney as an invader. They were instantly engaged in a bitter dogfight. When we got them apart, I learned that the Shepherd was Jim's dog! We finally trained them to keep a snarling distance from one another, but Jim and I did not dare make them share the same room with us during the ensuing year. Jim had already moved into our former room on the first floor. I was able to move Barney and me upstairs to a second-floor room shared very amicably with Fritz Post. My friendship with Jim remained over the years, but our dogs never learned to like each other. Surprisingly, they did get along peaceably with the four or five other dogs that joined their masters as fellow residents in the Beta House in my last year at Dartmouth.

Recreational Activity at Dartmouth

OWNING A CAR after the freshman year proved a great boon for weekends. The surrounding areas had mountains and hills for climbing, and forests, lakes, charming villages, and towns for rambling visits. My roadster with its main seat and rumble seat could accommodate me, Barney, three fellow students, and a picnic basket for lunch and many a sightseeing adventure. Sixty years ago there was still much evidence on the lower hillsides in middle New Hampshire and Vermont of fields formerly plowed and circumscribed by stone walls in various stages of disintegration, fields revealing the beginning of natural reforestation sprung from the uncultivated but forested higher hilltops.

Here and there we would come upon deserted farmhouses in various stages of disarray from dilapidated shutters, rotting shingled roofs, and collapsing walls all the way to a hollow basement, a receptacle holding the disintegrated detritus of what had once been a family home or barn. These remains embodied the shattered dreams of earlier generations of New England farmers who in the later nineteenth and earlier twentieth centuries abandoned much of this thin New England soil for the more promising opportunities in Ohio, Indiana, Michigan, Illinois, and still farther west. Even in my college days, one could still occasionally attend an auction at a farmhouse in the countryside or a village where household effects of old families were for sale in preparation for their departure elsewhere. At one of those auctions I bought an attractive antique desk and chair as well as some decorative pieces which, in the face of the still growing Depression, I subsequently virtually gave away at the end of my days at Dartmouth.

I had an opportunity to revisit some of this area in 1987 following the fifty-fifth reunion of the Dartmouth Class of 1932, when I drove from Hanover to the White Mountains. Close to the bank of an occasional river one might still see some cultivated green fields, some pastured cattle, white painted barns, and a house. But there were no traces of the stone walls visible from the car as we rode along. In the intervening years, the trees have marched down the hillsides and even the gentle slopes have covered most of the land with forest. Human habitations are visible only in towns or here and there in an occasional meadow beside a river.

At Dartmouth, I discovered in my freshman year another means of locomotion, one previously unknown to me and most people in my hometown of Chicago, namely skiing. Early on a Saturday morning in November 1928, we awoke to witness a heavy snowfall which gave every indication of continuing throughout the day. Four of us freshmen in Gile Hall got together to discuss what we should do. None of us owned skis, boots, or ski poles. One of our group had some background in skiing in Pennsylvania. Another from Massachusetts had been on skis twice. Two of us from Chicago, including me, had essentially never seen a pair of skis. We finally decided to go down to Main Street and buy the necessary equipment. We found the store inundated with customers. After what seemed like hours of waiting, we obtained the minimal necessary clothing, the proper boots, the ski poles and waxes, but not the skis. We were told to return in late afternoon, by which time the carpenter would have mounted the boot straps on the wooden skis.

By the time we were fully equipped, darkness was falling. We clumsily made our way to the Golf Clubhouse, the nearest hill to which we understood to be a preferred ski slope for practicing. There were no ski tows in those days, even in that ski pioneering area. Our resident expert from Pennsylvania described to the novices the herringbone technique. We laboriously made our way to the top of the hill. The one thing we knew about this hill was that there were no trees on it.

When the four of us had assembled at the top, our expert readied himself and headed down the slope. After silence, we heard a faint "Come on." The veteran of two previous times on skis positioned himself in the predecessor's tracks. As he disappeared, I decided I did not want to be left at the top alone, so I placed myself in the established track and waited for a faint cry from below. When it came, I shoved myself and went careening through the darkness. At one point, I shot up into the air, but came down on both skis. (I discovered later in the daylight that I had traversed a bunker beside a sand trap.) Somehow I reached the flat area on both skis. Our fourth member, who like me came from the flatlands around Chicago, somehow made it safely to the bottom. That night, the four of us laboriously made it to the top again, and miraculously repeated a second run. It was of course a stupid thing to do. The weather remained favorable for skiing for several days, and with advice and help from more experienced friends, I gradually learned to manipulate my skis, but for two weeks after that night's venture, I could not ski down that same hill in daytime without falling!

In the Hanover environment, I gradually turned from downhill skiing and the perfection of fast runs and found more pleasure in wintry cross-country skiing in the woods around Hanover accompanied by two or three friends and sometimes delightful chickadees. My skiing adventures after I left Dartmouth were confined to a couple of trips about 1940 from my residence in Urbana, Illinois, to the snowy area of northern Wisconsin and neighboring Michigan.

A further advantage of having a car was the possibility of easy access to an occasional weekend away from Hanover, if not in snowy and icy winter, at least in fall and spring. A Dartmouth football game with Harvard or Yale could be an occasion to load the car with friends for a weekend trip. Invitations to balls at Wellesley, Mount Holyoke, Vassar, or Smith could prompt a similar exodus. The Thanksgiving holiday might inspire a trip to my Uncle Edward's home in Montclair, New Jersey, or to Charlie Ryan's family home in Fall River. For a landlubber from the Middle West like me, it was an unusual thrill to have a weekend visit with Jim Moore and his family in Bayside, Long Island, where his father was commodore of the Yacht Club and had a 56–foot cruiser, on which we could enjoy a cruise.

For most of my undergraduate career, my parents had lovingly provided me with a comfortable allowance, though I do not think I was a lavish spender. One thing I did not spend money on was liquor. I had grown up in a household where my father, like his father before him, did not drink alcoholic beverages. But, even during Prohibition, he was at pains to have a supply of good liquors for serving to visiting friends. In that era of mixed drinks, he had some reputation as an amateur bartender. He even told me: if you do not want people at a party to know you are a teetotaler, volunteer to be a bartender. Prohibition was still in effect during my undergraduate years at Dartmouth, and the underground distribution of alcoholic beverages from Canada was evident in New Hampshire. So too was a certain amount of underground production of alcoholic concoctions by student amateurs at Dartmouth. I followed my father's advice, stayed away from liquor and preachment to others, and watched with sorrow the collapse of a bright and attractive alcoholic classmate, despite great effort by College officials to salvage him.

The Academic Curriculum at Dartmouth

AT THE OPENING of the fall term in September 1928, one of the first things an entering freshman did was appear at the Office of the President of Dartmouth College to be presented personally to President Ernest Martin Hopkins for a brief welcoming chat, and then be entered officially by the president as a member of the Class of 1932. This ceremony marked the beginning of one's being a Dartmouth man. It may have taken a little longer for the student to learn that Dr. Hopkins was not only a distinguished businessman who had been Vice President of AT&T, but a person who had become at Dartmouth a distinguished and creative educator. Before my graduation from Dartmouth, I would myself become a beneficiary of one of his subsequent but still enduring academic innovations, a Senior Fellowship. The latter is but one of many of his innovative actions as an educational statesman while president of Dartmouth.

In my freshman year, I took required courses in English and Math. After four years of Latin, and two years of French in high school, I continued with Latin and French in my freshman year. Two unusual but fascinating courses completed the menu: a one-semester course in Evolution followed by a one-semester course in Citizenship. They had relevance then and they could have relevance to life now.

Evolution was taught in a succession of lectures about astronomy, geology, physics, chemistry, and biology which provided students with some perspective on the physical environment. If such a course were taught in the 1990s, it might give a college undergraduate a broader overview of the natural world than the fragmented and narrowly specialized portions of science usually found in contemporary college instruction.

Citizenship, the other semester course required for all freshmen, was taught in small group discussion sessions led by professors generally drawn from social science departments. Content was derived from required readings dealing with actual issues confronting American citizens in the context of city, state, and federal government analysis and action. We students would soon face responsibilities as citizens in a democracy trying to analyze the pros and cons of social issues, and as voting citizens we would need to learn the views of others from diverse cultural backgrounds who were fellow citizens under the Constitution. We would have to search for compromises with them for our mutual welfare.

There was need for such a course in the 1920s. The availability of fast and cheaper steamships toward the end of the nineteenth century was accompanied by a boom in immigration, especially from Eastern Europe. The outbreak of bitter conflict among European nations in World War I had also produced some concern, particularly after American participation in that war, about the loyalty of some immigrants to the United States. Such concerns lay behind the actions of the Congress in passing laws in 1921 and again in 1924 which reduced the numbers of immigrants admissible particularly from specified countries. This bit of history provides some of the background for establishment of the course in Citizenship which I encountered as a freshman at Dartmouth in 1928.

Even my freshman courses ultimately exerted an influence on the direction of my future career. My fascination with Latin and its surrounding culture stirred by Augusta Stuart at Senn High School continued unabated under the influence of Professor Royal C. Nemiah, who taught a course on Latin poetry. It was further fueled by his offer several months into the year to meet with volunteers from the class one evening a week for sight reading of medieval Latin in an eleventh-century chronicle of the First Crusade. These sessions were held informally in the Nemiahs' home. There we met Mrs. Nemiah and a schoolboy son whom I was to encounter many years later as a professor of psychiatry at Harvard. In my freshman year I continued an interest in French and enjoyed particularly the second semester readings from the period of the French Revolution and Napoleonic Empire as taught by Professor Shirley Gale Patterson. He placed these literary works in the historical ambience of their times, and on the basis of his travels in France he enriched our awareness of the physical background of these events. As with the Nemiah family, I enjoyed visits to the home of the Pattersons. These generally took the form of invitations for dinner with the Pattersons, one or two other faculty persons, and a couple of students. These social occasions, supplemented by interesting experiences in contacts with professors in a variety of courses as an undergraduate, began to open my eyes to the pleasures and opportunities of an academic way of life.

In my freshman year, in addition to French and Latin and the required semester courses in Evolution and Citizenship, I took courses in English and Math. In my sophomore year, I continued the classical and Latin interest and turned also to German, Economics, Psychology, and Zoology. As a junior, I again studied Economics, added Sociology and Philosophy, and returned to Professor Nemiah for two year-long courses, Greek History and Classical Foundations of Modern Civilizations. In the first three years, my interests focused heavily on courses in the humanities and social sciences. These are fields of investigation which especially in Anglo-American speech have come to be regarded as concerned with the study of people, their culture, and their behavior, in contradistinction to the study of nature, the physical environment, which, particularly in the twentieth century, is blessed with designation as the intellectual domain of science and its offspring, technology. I shall return later more than once to the sad consequences of this unfortunate rift revealed in the language used in the intellectual world. Although I received a limited amount of instruction about the study of nature in my undergraduate years, I have always appreciated that unusual overview of scientific fields to which I was exposed in the required freshman course on evolution.

I have already commented on the way even in my freshman year Professors Nemiah and Patterson helped us enrich our understanding of the human situation presented in literary works by placing them in their historical and cultural settings. That same potential for breadth of perspective, for detecting cultural and social interrelationships in human and social behavior, was presented in other courses I encountered in my second and third college years. In later years, I wondered what could have been the source of this impression of abundant interrelations between disciplines. My best guess is that in 1928–32, Dartmouth College was a small and isolated community with few barriers to cross-disciplinary conversation among professors from different departments. Whatever the cause, I found the courses stimulating.

I had no anticipation of what was to befall me for my senior year. Among the many innovations of President Hopkins was the program for Senior Fellows. Beginning with the class of students who would graduate in 1930, five or six students at the end of their junior year were chosen to be Senior Fellows and thus relieved of all specific degree requirements. They were free to plan for their senior year their own program of intellectual activities using the resources of the College, the library, the laboratories, existing faculty courses or seminars, or specially designed instruction planned by a fellow in cooperation with individual faculty members.

In the early period that I am familiar with, there were no applications for Senior Fellowships to be submitted by students, but I believe that faculty members were requested to submit nominations. In my case, I was one of six appointees in the Class of 1932. We were free to approach any member of the faculty for advice and counsel. We could audit courses of our choice, and establish tutorial relationships. No official course or grade record was kept by the registrar.

At its beginning, my senior-year program had to be of my own devising, but it was conditioned especially by my experience in the first three years of college when I was exposed especially to various aspects of the Greek and Roman world. Under the able tutelage of Professor Williams, my attention was drawn to the final collapse of the Roman Empire and to an overview of the bloody interlude of the Merovingians, the salvaging of literary inheritances from ancient Greece and Rome in the Carolingian Renaissance and Empire, the shaping of the western kingdoms of Europe, the renewal of contact with the eastern Mediterranean in the Crusades of the eleventh to thirteenth centuries, and finally, the blending of the late Middle Ages into the Renaissance in the fourteenth and fifteenth centuries.

Professor Williams whetted my appetite for more of this fare while urging me to think of going to graduate school at Harvard to study for a Ph.D. in history under his maestro, Charles Homer Haskins, the preeminent medieval historian in the United States at that time. In view of such a possibility, I felt a need to expose myself to a broader array of history and I fortunately found well-taught courses in American and modern European history. I also had my eyes opened particularly about nonliterate societies by a course in anthropology. I audited a course in political science and in sociology. My senior year at Dartmouth was an eye-opener about human culture.

For the Christmas recess of my senior year in 1931, I returned to my family home in Glencoe. It was there in conversation with my father and mother that I broached with some hesitation the subject of my desire to acquire a Ph.D. from Harvard and to head for an academic career. It was not uncommon for relatives and friends to mention how my father had built his machine tool distribution business and to express expectations that I would one day become his successor. However, neither my father nor my mother had made such prophecies.

My father cleared the air immediately by saying that he had enjoyed his experiences in the Federal Machinery Sales Company, but that I had one life to live and I should live it my way in accord with my own desires and decisions. He added that he did have to inform me more completely about the devastating decline in profitability of the machine tool business in the enduring Depression. His situation was worse than I had known, and I was appalled by the thought of money I had spent from my allowance in the previous year for some expenditures that I might have avoided. I resolved then that if I were to head for a graduate program at Harvard, it would have to be without financial assistance from my family.

But first I would have to gain admission to the Harvard Graduate School. I submitted the necessary application form, and my Dartmouth professors sent in their recommendations. Lo and behold, I learned that Dartmouth had some endowed funds to support three or four Dartmouth graduates for a first year of graduate education. In due course, I was admitted to the Harvard Graduate School for the fall of 1932, and I was awarded a $1,000 fellowship from Dartmouth College.

To help matters, a Harvard undergraduate and I were both able to get two-month summer jobs with Butler Brothers, a Chicago-based corporation that sold home and clothing goods through a catalogue and a chain of stores similar to the operation of Sears Roebuck. The buyers in charge of the subdivisions of merchandise appearing in their main catalogue had marked the items and the related bargain prices to be listed in a new special bargain catalogue. We two college students were to produce a draft for the text, presumably by the end of two months. My colleague and I of course met the chief buyers for each of the sections in the course of working on the catalogue.

Our work was boring enough that we completed our job early in the second month. Instead of being terminated at that point, each of us was assigned to a buyer. I worked immediately with the buyer for Department Y, cosmetics and household items, then the most profitable department in the company and under the management of a very capable man. At the end of the month, he asked me to continue working with him at Butler Brothers. I declined, leaving with my two months' pay, which helped to pay my way to Boston and the Harvard Graduate School. So I missed a chance to make myself somebody important in the merchandising world!

The Path Is Set:
Graduate Education
at Harvard,
1932–1934

WITH THE FUNDS FROM THE DARTMOUTH FELLOWSHIP, savings from my summer employment, and proceeds from the sale of my car, I entered my first year, the 1932–33 year, in the Harvard Graduate School, with the $400 tuition paid and the intention to live that year as economically as possible. My classmate and good friend over four years at Dartmouth, Charles Ryan, was also entering Harvard, as a Law School student. We rented together a cheap two-room suite on the top floor of an old Victorian rooming house a short distance from Harvard Yard, the Law School, and cheap places to eat. We both kept our noses in books when we were not in class, but enjoyed an occasional weekend at the Ryan family home in Fall River.

In the same rooming house we encountered two congenial law students, Gaither Jenkins from North Carolina and Paul Palmer from Ohio. Toward the end of the academic year the four of us decided to look for a cheap two-bedroom apartment we might share. We found one just off Massachusetts Avenue and several blocks from the Harvard Square area, which we leased for the 1933–34 year.

We jointly rented a meager supply of used—I should say, abused—furniture. The kitchen presented opportunities for preparing meals in the apartment at some additional savings. It is difficult to convey to a later generation the feeling of changing expectations during the Depression, which witnessed the closing of the banks and the forty percent devaluation of the dollar in foreign exchange. Since my fellowship from Dartmouth was not renewable for a second year, I had tried to save as much as possible toward my second-year expenses.

Fortunately, I was able to get a job in the summer of 1933 working for Sears Roebuck, which had recently added a life insurance branch to its Allstate auto insurance business by purchasing the troubled National Life Insurance Company of Illinois, then located at 11 South LaSalle Street in Chicago's Loop. Sears was in the process of moving National Life's offices to its complex of buildings west of the Loop. The insurance company had, like most such companies in the 1930s, acquired an enormous quantity of bulky records, which were stored in transfer cases and card files.

I found myself one of four husky brutes assigned the job of preparing these records, in a large basement area, for transfer to the Sears complex, presumably under the supervision of the office manager. His lack of performance helped explain the difficulties besetting the life insurance company. It fell to me to analyze the shelving spaces allocated to the life insurance operation in the Sears space and to develop a code system for marking the individual cases. It took much of the summer to do the necessary coding of the cases for transfer to designated filing spaces in the new offices. Near the end of August the actual transfer was handled by professional movers with my colleagues and me guiding the placement of files at the new site. At completion I was told to report to the Sears officer in charge of the insurance business.

He was very friendly and appreciative, and asked if I would be interested in working for Sears. It was a great temptation because I was still very worried about financing the second year of graduate school. But I decided to persevere at Harvard with savings from the first year and my summer wages, which provided about $150. I borrowed $200 from Mr. Marsilius, and returned it to him a couple of years later. It was my extreme good fortune to receive a $400 scholarship grant from Harvard for the 1933–34 year, which in effect waived the tuition fee for that year. I survived my second year as a graduate student at Harvard in the depths of the Depression with the least amount of money ever. I remember that I went many days without breakfast but had a 15-cent lunch consisting of a glass of milk and a sandwich from Hazen's and the 35-cent special evening bargain at a cheap restaurant much frequented by students.

It must be said that while my second year at Harvard was financially my most difficult one, I was far from being the only impecunious student during this desperate time when even the banks closed. I was fortunate to share accommodations in a rooming house and then an apartment with congenial fellows—Ryan, Jenkins, and Palmer. Their days were spent as law students in the Law School buildings while I was occupied in the classroom buildings and Widener Library within the Harvard Yard. Since I became involved in my first year at Harvard in a course on the origins of the English common law in the Middle Ages, my roommates kept me informed about visiting speakers at the Law School. My occasional attendance whetted an interest that led me in later years to some intellectual activity about law.

Intellectual Fare for a Harvard Graduate Student

I ENTERED HARVARD in 1932 presumptively as a candidate for a graduate degree in history at a singularly fortunate time. History was a favored subject then even by undergraduates. In the 1930s hardly a single freshman escaped Harvard's bombastic Roger Bigelow Merriman's lecture course on Europe: History 1. There were many undergraduate students majoring in history with a growing expansion of interest beyond the West to include the East and Latin America.

While I was never to see the great medievalist Charles Homer Haskins, a home-bound invalid who died during my first year at Harvard, there was a galaxy of distinguished older professors whom I had the good fortune to contact personally in various ways, either enrolled in courses or seminars or in a few cases as an auditor: Charles Howard McIlwain, George LaPiana, Gaetano Salvemini, William Scott Ferguson, Arthur Darby Nock, Sidney Bradshaw Fay, Samuel Eliot Morison, and Arthur Meier Schlesinger, Sr. The plenitude of distinguished scholarly and teaching talent at more junior ranks had been encouraged by President Lowell's inauguration of the student tutorial program in conjunction with the student House program. I encountered such teachers and counselors as Charles Holt Taylor, Crane Brinton, Gaines Post, Michael Karpovich, Mason Hammond, and Paul Buck.

In retrospect I realize that I carried from my undergraduate experience at Dartmouth a certain orientation into my graduate experience at Harvard. In my freshman year at Dartmouth, Professor Patterson had a way of placing French literary works into their larger cultural setting, and by my junior year Professor Nemiah had expanded teaching about Latin literature into an approach to classical civilization whose decline and fall left a residue of important consequence for the Middle Ages in Europe and for the orientation of historians of the Middle Ages like myself.

One of the things about medieval history that has intrigued me is that to an unusual degree medievalists tend to look at past history in terms of a multiple set of categories. For later periods one finds many kinds of historians, such as economic or political or literary historians, or historians of art. The Medieval Academy of America attracts all brands of historians to its meetings, and the preferred journal for articles on the Middle Ages of whatever category is its *Speculum*. At least my generation of American medieval historians tended to share a broad interest in many aspects of medieval civilization and culture.

Such a diversity is reflected in my choice of courses at Harvard in 1932–34. They focused largely on Western Europe and embodied a mix of lectures, readings, discussions, and occasionally a written essay. Under McIlwain I studied the constitutional history of England to the sixteenth century, and then the history of political theory. Under Taylor I studied medieval institutions, the history of France to 1461, and the intellectual history of Europe, 500 to 1300. I studied the history of the Roman Republic under Ferguson, of the Roman Empire under Hammond, and of Italy under LaPiana. Important skills for a medieval historian were made available to me and a few fellow students in a very useful seminar taught by Post entitled Elements of Latin Palaeography and Diplomatics with Reference to the Use of Historical Sources.

I did depart from the ancient, medieval, and Renaissance terrain during my first two years of course work at Harvard by enrolling in Brinton's lively course on the intellectual history of Europe, 1750–1850. I also attended with some frequency lectures in courses on colonial America by Samuel Morison, on the Civil War by Paul Buck, and on more recent America by Arthur Schlesinger, Sr.

There were certain showcase academic events which could entice as visitors graduate students as well as others. Roger Merriman's delivery of his lectures in the European history course during the 1930s captured virtually the entire freshman class. When he reached the day when he described in his lecture the event in which the Emperor Henry IV made humble submission to pope Gregory VII at Canossa, numerous visitors could be expected to try to gain admission to the lecture hall.

A somewhat smaller group of auditors were attracted to the opening of a course on the Renaissance. Some graduate students had named this course the "Three Ring Circus" because the three professors who presented it disagreed among themselves on what date should be used to indicate the beginning of the Renaissance. The historian (again Merriman) argued that the story of the Renaissance should begin about 1250, reflecting the collapse of imperial power after the death of Frederick I. The literary scholar argued that it should begin about 1350, with the period following Dante's death.

The art historian favored 1450, marking completion of the Cathedral of Florence dome. Despite this peccadillo, the triumvirate offered a lively presentation of the history, culture, and arts of the Italian Renaissance.

If one combines the list of courses I took as an undergraduate at Dartmouth with those I took at Harvard as a graduate student, it becomes evident that by 1934 I had devoted the major portion of my attention to the human history of Europe in the Greek and Roman periods, the Middle Ages, and the Renaissance.

A particular incident toward the end of my first year as a graduate student aroused my interest in the active investigation of historical evidence itself. In his year-long course on Constitutional History of England to the Sixteenth Century, Professor McIlwain directed our attention to the words in specific historical documents which were usually in Latin, and, in the present instance, were associated with the emergence in England of the common law and the use of juries in the twelfth and thirteenth centuries.

Each student had a printed book of relevant texts and a glossary of established translations in English. The king's judges, as they moved about the realm and encountered complaints of one subject against another, began to impanel juries of persons sworn to tell the judge the truth about the facts alleged in the complaints. A person chosen to be a juror could be described as a *liber et legalis homo*.

By the time I was a student at Harvard both adjectives had been translated for several centuries by historians to mean "free men." When I expressed my feeling that this translation did not seem reasonable, McIlwain, characteristically, urged me to investigate the matter and write a course paper. I did find evidence in the sources that *liber* meant a free man in contradistinction to a serf or unfree man, but that *legalis* meant a person who was lawful, law-abiding, and thus oath-worthy, and to be trusted to speak the truth as a juror. Thus even a person who was not free, but who was judged to have a lawful record, to be *legalis*, might participate in a jury summoned by the judges. McIlwain urged me to submit my paper on *legalis homo* to *Speculum*, where it ultimately appeared in print in eight pages in the April 1940 issue as my first published "learned article."

As we graduate students at Harvard in 1934 neared the end of our second year of organized course instruction, we anticipated spending the next semester or two in more individual study to prepare for a general examination for the Ph.D. degree conducted by five faculty historians. In midmorning very near the end of the spring term, I encountered at the entrance to the classroom for McIlwain's political theory course a fellow-student who was to become a lifelong friend, Myron Gilmore. He showed me a letter he had received that morning stating that the History Department had recently reviewed the requirement that all graduate students, after at least two years of course work, take a general examination for the Ph.D., and had decided that the examination could be waived in some cases by vote of the department, in view of the breadth and depth already achieved by the candidate. In such cases the candidate could turn directly to working on his thesis. Of course I congratulated Myron on his good fortune. When I returned to my quarters later that day, I found a similar letter addressed to me.

When I began at Harvard, the established medieval historians in America were involved mostly in studying the western European peoples of the eleventh to the fourteenth centuries—a feudal age, a time when it was difficult to fuse local political lords into larger stable structures. A commanding figure among American medievalists was Harvard's Charles Homer Haskins. Shortly before my arrival at Harvard he became a bedridden invalid and soon died.

A youngish man as an associate professor, Charles Holt Taylor, a remarkably conscientious person of substantial ability, was asked to take over Haskins's medieval territory. He did so with better intellectual command of the subject than he, I believe, admitted to himself. While his publications were few, despite his long years at Harvard, his lectures and conversations with students in my experience were full of meat. Now that I had to focus on a potential

Ph.D. thesis subject, I found myself influenced by my respect for Taylor and fascinated by his subject matter. I began to focus on the story of the emergence of the feudal structure of European society in the eleventh to thirteenth centuries. Fortunately for me, Taylor agreed to be my thesis sponsor. I was to learn from him that there was only one way to put together a thesis: get it right.

It quickly became evident from my conversations with Taylor and other faculty members that my historical investigation of western European culture in the Middle Ages would really require of me, as an American, a citizen of the New World, some exposure to the surviving monuments and material artifacts of the Old World's Middle Ages, as well as access to medieval documents and manuscripts in European archives and libraries. Through reading about medieval architecture, I had already acquired some understanding of the reasons behind particular styles expressed in European castles and churches. I had also developed some skill in reading a rare parchment document in an American library, but more often a printed version of early documents preserved in volumes published from the sixteenth century to the present and available to me in the Harvard Library.

But this was the spring of 1934—still the depths of the Depression. My father's business was at its lowest ebb. My parents were therefore unable to assist me financially. Then came one of the miracles of my life, surely instigated by Taylor and other Harvard faculty, the news that Harvard had granted me a traveling fellowship for $1,000 and a waiver of tuition for the upcoming 1934–35 academic year.

It soon became evident that a major focus of my attention should be France, starting with Paris and the great manuscript collections in its Archives Nationales and its Bibliothèque Nationale, as well as the plenitude of surviving castles, cathedrals, and churches in its environs. I soon found that in the thirties the cheapest and most pleasant voyage to Europe was by way of the Arnold Bernstein Line, whose ships carried one class of passengers on the upper decks and American automobiles chained to the lower decks—not boxed in the ship's hold, as was the practice of other shipping lines. The Bernstein ships could load and unload more quickly than competitors and maintain a more stable arrival and departure schedule. I purchased for $150 a round-trip ticket on the Bernstein Line traveling between New York and Antwerp.

A Harvard
Fellow Abroad,
1934–1935

MY PARENTS DROVE ME TO NEW YORK AND TO THE
Bernstein Line ship *Ilsenstein*, which I boarded on September 23,
1934, with about sixty others including one good friend, fellow
Harvard graduate student Myron Gilmore. Already chained to the
flooring of the lower decks were 406 American-made automobiles
for delivery to Antwerp. The summer's flood of travelers to Europe
had abated and all the single passengers aboard could have a cabin
to themselves. Perhaps a quarter of the passengers were Americans,
and most of the rest were Europeans from many different countries. Both the open deck and the interior recreational areas provided welcoming spaces for conversation and games. The dining
room was pleasant, the food good if not fancy, and the tables just
large enough to facilitate conversation.

The speed of the ship was at a maximum fifteen knots, and the
first days were clear and sunny. The young captain obviously liked
having passengers aboard and took pains to entertain us. One day
he spotted a small three-masted sailing ship, and slightly altered
course to bring us closer to view it and wave to the Italian crew. He

took to giving a short blast on the whistle to bring us out on deck to see anything notable, like a large number of enormous whales broaching the surface of the sea, or porpoises cavorting about the bow of our ship. As the weather began to change and threatening clouds appeared, a blast of the whistle brought us near the bridge to see the captain pointing the ship toward the middle of an enormous but perfect half-circle of a rainbow. This was the prelude to a vast and dangerous storm that greatly slowed our progress even though it approached us from astern. At one point we passed the big westbound liner *Majestic*, a frightening sight as it bore down upon a huge wave, then seemed to heave up and pour from its decks back into the ocean a mass of white water. Somewhat later a blast of the whistle brought us to the bridge area again. At first we saw nothing but the peaks and valleys of the waves. Then, as if by the hand of Neptune, a two-masted fishing ship lifted on the crest of a wave. It seemed to be surviving the storm, and we passed on.

The storm had abated by the time we passed the south coast of Britain and headed up the Channel toward Antwerp, where we landed at the end of the first week in October 1934. This lengthened voyage provided Myron and me with opportunities to make friends with some Americans and Europeans with whom we could have pleasant encounters in our European adventure, beginning with sightseeing in Antwerp itself. Though Myron and I expected to make Paris our base, we took advantage of landing in Antwerp to see in Belgium and the Netherlands some of the many material heritages and monuments from the Middle Ages and Renaissance. One of our shipboard companions was an excellent guide to Antwerp itself, setting a precedent which was to be repeated subsequently by other such friends in this year abroad.

Myron and I passed from Antwerp to Ghent and Bruges, and then moved north into the Netherlands, going first to the Isle of Walcheren, a rich and picturesque farming scene, and then to Amsterdam. A Dutch engineering professor, who had been a visiting lecturer in North Carolina, arranged for us to meet his younger brother, a medical student at the University of Leiden, and to stay with him in student lodgings. The older brother was then our host to see The Hague and Delft. We then left for Belgium's capital, Brussels, where we were wonderfully received by an American shipmate and her family living there. After several days spent seeing the environs of Brussels, Myron and I took the train, inevitably in third class, to Paris.

My Base in Paris

MYRON HAD HEARD good things about the Villa des Fleurs, a rooming house with food service at Rue d'Assas in the 6th Arrondissement. It proved attractive and Myron made arrangements to make it his Paris base. Since the cost was too much for my lean budget, I decided to seek an alternative. While I was still in Cambridge I had heard about a French professorial family, the Tramonds, who had a spare room in a large apartment which had become the Paris quarters for a succession of Harvard graduate students who later became faculty members, such as Paul Buck, Donald McKay, Gaines Post, and Everett Gleason. The Harvard group offered to send the Tramonds a letter of sponsorship, but fearing that the cost of the room and meals would be too high for me, I felt I must decline. Fortunately, they insisted on giving me a letter of introduction to the Tramonds.

I did not know that they subsequently provided a sponsoring letter for a fellow graduate student who was to become a good friend of mine, Edwin Popper. He arrived in Paris some time before I did, and made a resolute effort to reach the Tramonds in their apartment, but to no avail. Again I was to be blessed by a kind of miraculous intervention. The Tramonds' oldest daughter had become very ill and died soon after. The entire family had left Paris to bury her remains in the Tramond family plot near their ancestral home in Correze, in central France. Meanwhile Popper, unable to make contact with the family, had found a pleasant room, amazingly with a full private bath, in a small hotel that happened to be next door to the building containing the Tramond apartment.

When the Tramond family finally returned to Paris, they had no messages from Popper and no knowledge of his whereabouts. Meanwhile I was in need of shelter and appeared out of the blue with a letter of introduction. We talked, became friendly, and I confessed my concerns about the financial aspects. They proposed a small reduction, and I accepted and moved in the next day as a very lucky person. A few days later Popper, now happy with his accommodations, made contact with the Tramonds and found me there. A delightful person, he was liked by the Tramond family, and was a guest on frequent occasions. It turned out that Popper's window was on the same level and immediately adjacent to the Tramond apartment windows, with a ledge that permitted the Tramond cat to walk over to Popper's window for tidbits. For reasons I shall explain later, by a different route I went in the reverse direction when I needed a bath.

The Tramond apartment was at 46 rue Jacob, an east-west street which parallels — a long city block to the north — the boulevard bordering the south bank of the Seine. On the opposite bank lay the royal palace and gardens of the Louvre. Only a block away to the east from the Tramond apartment was the Church of St. Germain des Prés, the only visible survivor of what had been the lands of the monastery of that name founded in the sixth century. By the seventeenth century, French royal power had tamed the local feudal aristocracy and made participation in the courtly life of the royal palace a more attractive style of life than was available in their isolated hilltop castles.

By the seventeenth century these aristocrats were buying pieces of the monastic lands south of the Louvre to build elegant town houses, many of which survive today as apartment buildings like the one at 46 rue Jacob. In the center of the facade on the street was a large gated opening for a horse and rider, horse-drawn carriage, automobile, or pedestrians, which led to a small inner square flanked by projections from the building's front section, facing the street. A circular staircase provided access to four apartment levels topped by an attic divided into small private rooms for household servants from the apartments. The ceiling height at the first level up was distinctly higher than on the third level, where I was to live with the Tramond family.

The staircase doorway to their apartment opened into a reception room beyond which to the right was the *cabinet*, an enclosure for the only flush toilet in the apartment. To the left of it a hallway extended the width of the apartment. A door on the left, also within the reception room, led into a spacious dining room with a window onto the enclosed court. A door on its opposite wall gave entrance to my room, which also had a window onto the court. It was a pleasant room with a bed, writing table and chair, reading chair, chest, and handsome fireplace, the only means of heating the room.

In an adjoining alcove with a door into the central hallway was a rack for towels. A small table supported toilet articles, a large pitcher of cold water, and a bowl for washing hands and face. Early each morning Jeanne, the family maid recruited from a peasant family in Correze, replenished for me the cold water in the pitcher and provided for shaving a small amount of hot water heated in a tank connected to the coal-fired kitchen range. Each day she also emptied my bucket filled with waste water. I could use that single toilet off the reception hall along with all of the Tramond family, but there were no facilities for bathing available to me.

I did learn subsequently that there was a sizable tank of heated water at the top of the kitchen stove which could drain into a hollow metal ring with holes on the bottom side through which water could flow. When the ring was placed on the shoulders, a placid stream of water reached the body of the member of the family who was standing with his or her feet in a circular metal pan. I learned that Saturday mornings were reserved for this family ritual. It seemed that I would have to do my bathing in one of the big public baths on barges in the Seine. Or, still more expensive, for a fee I could use briefly a bathroom in a hotel. Fortunately for me, Ed

Popper was discovered living happily in the hotel next door in a room with its own full bath. With consummate grace, he immediately proposed that I should use his private bath as needed. It is no wonder that my friendship for him has endured for decades.

As I have said, the Tramonds' oldest child, a daughter in her twenties, had died in September 1934, shortly before my arrival in Paris. There were four children in the family when I joined it in October. The two daughters, in their later teens, Violaine and Simone, were friendly but somewhat reserved in manner, as befitted proper French families then. The two boys, Michel and Martial, were in their early teens. All conversation in the house was in French, in casual conversation as well as at the luncheon and dinner table. My comprehension of spoken French on my arrival was substantially better than my ability to speak French with any fluidity.

The children were wonderfully helpful in correcting my faulty speech in casual conversation when we were alone. Michel, the older boy, had reached the age when he liked in the evening to hear what was going on outside on the streets of Paris because of the growing political agitation and public demonstrations at that time. Besides correcting my spoken French, he also enjoyed trying to teach me at least some of the current French slang. I am sure his parents would have been shocked and angered by his efforts to teach me street language, but this remained a secret between Michel and me. More important to me, he remained quick to help me correct my spoken proper French.

In the Tramond household breakfast for me was a simple affair of coffee with hot milk, rolls, and some fruit brought to my room by the ever present maid, Jeanne. With the two-hour noon break typical in Paris then, a leisurely hour-long luncheon with conversation and a substantial menu was common. In the Tramond household one or two guests could be invited to luncheon, relatives or friends of the Tramond family, and gradually a number of acquaintances of mine whom the Tramonds also came to enjoy.

The mother of the family, Mme. Tramond, was a tremendously capable, matronly, and lovable person. She stayed within her own French culture linguistically, but somehow she could communicate feelingly with others like the Americans I had introduced to her. She liked art and advised me on visits to a number of exhibits I would have missed. She followed the news of ecclesiastical musical events in cathedrals and churches which I sometimes attended with her. She revealed to me everyday aspects of French family life by occasionally taking me on shopping trips that opened my eyes to a culture in some respects very different from what I had known. She was at the same time a nurturing mother to her children, and she had obviously earned the gratitude and respect of my Harvard predecessors who had been taken into the family at 46 rue Jacob. She certainly earned my lifelong gratitude.

In contrast to the easy manner of Madame Tramond, M. Joannes Tramond was polite and correct, consistent with his style of dress. He always wore a formal black suit and shoes, a white shirt with a high circular collar without wings but with a formal black tie, and his hair was carefully combed down. To top it off, he consistently wore a glass monocle which I believe was associated in some way with a visual impairment. On first impression he might have seemed formidable. While on a few occasions he revealed anger or disagreement, there was an unruffled politeness about him that reflected kindness.

He was a respected historian of the French Navy and the French colonies. At the time of his unexpected death he was already a likely candidate for the Collège de France, the highest possible appointment for a French professor. He was helpful to me with introductions to some of the top French professors in medieval studies. Behind that formal manner was a very intelligent and kind and helpful person. It was clear that my American acquaintances who met the Tramonds liked Madame Tramond and respected M. Tramond, and were pleased to be invited guests in their home. I remain enormously indebted to them for their kindness to me and their tutelage of me.

Archives in Paris

DURING MY FELLOWSHIP year in Europe I made no effort to undertake any courses or seminars at universities, though I took advantage of the occasional public lectures and opportunities for conversation with professors. Somehow M. Tramond did manage to obtain for me a seat for the opening exercises of the University of Paris. In a letter to my parents in mid-November I wrote as follows:

Saturday afternoon I attended the opening exercises of the University of Paris. It was a gay pageant for color. The robes were bright reds and yellows trimmed with white fur. I felt a thrill in attending this exercise at the oldest university in the world. French savants, however, can make just as boring speeches as Americans. The deans of the four faculties (Law, Medicine, Sciences, Letters) spoke and finally the rector (president), Charlety. The latter's speech was very good but it was not cheerful. The audience was made pretty gloomy, for Charlety referred to contemporary conditions in France.

From the perspective of more than sixty years later, we Americans can be sympathetic to the French who were also facing depression and internal political turmoil, not to speak of their growing fear of Nazi Germany.

As already noted above, the primary objectives of my fellowship year abroad were twofold: to see the surviving material evidence of the imprint of the European medieval past on its contemporary culture, and to become more acquainted with the written records of the Middle Ages in archives and libraries. My extended stay at a base in Paris was attributable to the mass of important records of the eleventh through thirteenth centuries available in the Archives Nationales and the Bibliothèque Nationale. Both of these institutions were within walking distance from the Tramond residence, easy for the Bibliothèque, strenuous for the Archives, but just possible for a twenty-three year old, though the closing of these institutions from noon to 2 P.M. to permit the traditional leisurely lunch often required two round trips per day.

From late October 1934 to late January 1935, I concentrated on the documents at the Archives.

They were all written by hand, often in a style in varying degrees similar to contemporary printing, and mostly in Latin with occasional pieces in a vernacular tongue. They could open up vistas of well-known historical figures and fascinating unknowns who emerged as individuals from the words inscribed on these parchment pages.

Fatigued eyes could of course force me to leave the scrutiny of documents in order to use a day or an afternoon for visiting the environs of Paris to see an ancient castle, a cathedral or church, an ancient village, a royal palace or hunting lodge—sites offering their own historical testimony about the human past.

On my birthday, January 10, 1935, I received some wonderful news about the ensuing 1935–36 year in a letter from Harvard granting a waiver of the tuition charge for that year and a $1,000 assistantship for the Radcliffe version of History 1, European History, the lecturers being Charles Taylor in the first semester and Sidney Fay in the second. Though feeling secure about financial support for the year ahead, I was concerned about funding for travel in Europe which I hoped to do in the spring and early summer of 1935. Fortunately I was able to borrow $200 from a family friend, whom I repaid with interest the following year. By then my father's business had also begun its recovery.

By mid-January 1935, I had transferred my attention to the historical materials in the Bibliothèque Nationale. Writers and historians as far back as the 1600s had begun to make printed copies of medieval handwritten records some of which were subsequently lost or destroyed in wars. These collections have their utility also for modern historians, as do the narratives of earlier historians found in the Bibliothèque. By mid-February, I had met in Paris William Jones, a Dartmouth graduate in 1933 who had come to France to obtain a doctoral degree in French literature from the Sorbonne and who wished to continue archival studies in Vienna. He urged me to join him in a brief swing across southern Germany to Vienna, where he would remain while after a few days I would return to France.

My mentor from Harvard, Charles Taylor, arrived in France at that moment, and he urged me to make that swing with Jones. It was at this very time that M. Tramond took ill with pneumonia and died. Mme. Tramond agreed that I could continue to regard her apartment as my base for a few months while making a series of short trips to the French provinces to see historical monuments and visit some public regional archival collections.

An Interlude in Germany

BUT FIRST BILL JONES and I were to make a detour through Germany to Vienna. Early on a Tuesday morning, March 12, we left by train for Strasbourg, where we saw its beautiful cathedral in the afternoon. Then we took the train to Nuremburg, a city rich in medieval structures, finally reaching Munich on Friday evening, March 15, 1935. Jones and I spent Saturday sightseeing in the center of Munich, and for the equivalent of fifty cents we bought seats in the top gallery of the Opera House for the evening performance of Wagner's *The Flying Dutchman*.

As we left the house, we found a large crowd gathered in the square where special copies of the Nazi newspaper were being distributed. Bill and I obtained copies and returned to our hotel to read them. We learned that Hitler had renounced the military clauses of the Versailles Treaty forbidding the rearming of Germany—clauses he had already defied. The following Sunday morning trucks loaded with German troops went through the streets of Munich distributing handbills to the populace, one of which I still have. It was headed, "Munich greets the Führer." It affirmed, "Germany has the universal obligation for military service," and urged the populace to hoist the banners, decorate their houses, come out into the streets, and at four in the afternoon greet Hitler.

That Sunday, March 17, climaxed a beautiful spring weekend

which had pulled the people of Munich out-of-doors in their regional garb into the woods and countryside, but a great throng had gathered by midafternoon along the boulevards which constituted Hitler's line of march through the city. Bill and I returned to the site of our previous evening's entertainment, the Opera House Square. We found ourselves standing in a dense crowd but close to the curb and to the place where Hitler's open touring car would have to slow down to make a sharp left turn. The crowd had waited patiently behind the line of black-uniformed troops who stood in the street itself but near the curbing.

As the crowd became restive, individuals began to push forward a little to see farther into the line of approach of Hitler's party. Several times an officer of rather small stature standing farther into the street shouted, "Back, Back," and the crowd moved backward. Once again there was a small push forward, and this time the officer, looking very angry, quickly moved beyond his soldiers into the crowd. He not only shouted at three Bavarians in their *lederhosen* but gave the big fellow standing between me and the curb a shove. The physically impressive Bavarian turned on the little officer in an overpowering manner and shouted at him in German, "What do you think we are, Prussians?"

This verbal blast was sufficient to send the officer into the street safely behind his line of troops. I was later to be told by Bavarians that this was an instance of civil courage more likely to appear among Bavarians than Prussians. Some minutes later the rising level of shouting and cheering announced the approach of an open touring car not more than thirty feet away from me, as it slowly made a right angle turn toward the Isar River. Hitler was clearly visible, standing in the rear of the vehicle and waving triumphantly to the surrounding populace.

This incident was sufficient to awaken in me a real curiosity about what was going on in Germany and to arouse a desire for opportunities to talk with Germans about their situation. While this thought was germinating, Bill and I used the remainder of a week for sightseeing, attending two more operas and a symphony concert, and sampling the beer halls and cafés. By the end of the week in Munich I had decided not to go to Vienna but to go instead to the nearest Austrian city, Salzburg, where I could buy at a very cheap rate the German marks I would need for an inexpensive stay in Munich. Fortunately for me I was able to make up for the brevity of my visit to Salzburg in 1935 by month-long stays in August 1956 and 1961 as a lecturer about American universities in the Salzburg Seminar in American Studies.

Given my happy experience with the Tramond family in Paris, I hoped I might find a German family in Munich who would shelter an American student. In that first week in Munich I had encountered its American Library. I went there and indeed found a list of such households and an elderly, gracious countess who was familiar with the list. She had apparently had happy experiences on visits to the United States, and was very friendly. She recommended that I go to see Frau Major Sammiller at Habsburgerstrasse 8/0.

On March 25, 1935, I wrote a letter home which began by citing the Sammiller address as currently my new address and saying:

Fortune continues to smile upon me, for this is a wonderful home to be in. It is in an excellent location in Munich, near enough to the center of town, a short walk to the Staatsbibliotek, and a short walk to the chief park of Munich, the English Garden.

The apartment itself had spacious rooms, admirably furnished with historic pieces of furniture and with paintings of ancestors back at least to the sixteenth century. My own room was a beautiful example. My suits and other clothing were kept in a huge, tall chest, a wedding gift from the seventeenth century.

When I rang the bell at the entrance to the Sammiller apartment, the door was opened by a maid in uniform who understood my halting German enough to lead me to the drawing room and to Frau Sammiller, a tall and gracious woman who, fortunately for me, added to German an excellent command of spoken French, in which she explained to me that she and her husband had started taking into their family enclave student English speakers to encourage the learning of spoken English by her two sons. For some reason, the American student who had begun the academic year with the Sammillers had to leave, creating a vacancy for me. I could not have had better older friends and advisers than Mme. Tramond and Frau Sammiller.

Frau Sammiller's husband was Herr Major Sammiller, a young officer in the German Army during World War I, whose professional career had been terminated at the end of that war by the provisions of the Versailles Treaty, which forbade Germany to have an army. The former officers of the Bavarian portion of the German Army had formed a self-help organization of which Major Sammiller was the chief administrator. He proved very friendly to me and helped me improve my spoken German at the time of my stay with the family.

Frau Sammiller, herself of aristocratic background, had first been married to Freiherr von Rehlingen, their oldest child being a daughter who, at the time I was in Munich, was married to a Prussian aristocrat and living in northeastern Germany. Their second child was a son, Fritz, now Freiherr von Rehlingen, who at the time of my stay with the family was in his early twenties and a student of history at the University of Munich. He and I were to have a long-lasting friendship. After a divorce from her first husband and marriage with Major Sammiller, Frau Sammiller had a son, now eighteen years old, named Raimund Sammiller, a very attractive young fellow whose life would end at Stalingrad.

Luncheon and dinner were served in the spacious dining room with opportunities for conversation in German. It was common practice after dinner for the Sammillers, Fritz, and me to adjourn to the drawing room where a maid would distribute to each of us a glass of wine. The maid would then leave the room, closing the double doors. We listened to the click of her heels on the tile down the central hall as she walked to the door opening into the servant's area. As a response to silence, Herr Sammiller would start the conversation by asking me what I had learned from the Paris *Herald* or other English-language newspapers I had seen that day in the American Library. Hitler's recent open renunciation of the terms of the Versailles Treaty restraining Germany's rearmament had sparked a major debate among the nations which was reflected in the press outside Germany. Herr Sammiller himself regularly bought a copy of the German-language newspaper published in Basle, Switzerland, but it was more likely to be suppressed by the Hitlerian government authorities than English-language newspapers.

It was evident that the Sammillers were worried by the belligerent Hitler and his impact on Germany and the world. In Catholic Bavaria in 1935, there was some dissonance about the Hitler regime. While living with the Sammillers I took my personal laundry to a nearby shop served by elderly women who, on my first entry, received me with a Nazi greeting to which I responded, "Grüsse Gott." In subsequent returns to that shop I was greeted instantly with "Grüsse Gott!" On another occasion, when I entered a small barber shop late in the afternoon for a haircut, one barber was at the point of leaving but the other was obviously almost finished with an elderly gentleman and he waived me toward an empty barber chair. After escorting the old man to the door, bowing respectfully and saying farewell, he turned to me, and seeing my gray tweed outfit, which must have made me look like a fellow German, he rattled off in German, "They shot his son, they shot his son!"

I guessed what he meant, because I had seen a recent newspaper item reporting that a young man's riddled body had been found in a roadside ditch near Munich. The victim was the leader in Bavaria of a large Catholic youth organization which had remained outside the Hitler Youth movement. An even more open incident of anti-Nazi talk occurred on a Munich streetcar when a group of younger people were exchanging jokes at the expense of Hitler and the Nazis. But I too could be taught to be careful. While dining with the Sammillers in a restaurant near their villa in Partenkirchen, I was in the course of making a remark critical about the Hitler regime when I felt Herr Sammiller tap my knee, thus silencing me. I realized that at that moment a couple of persons were

My mother, Mary Cord Odegaard.

With my sister, Marjorie, and my mother, ca. 1930.

With my new Chrysler open roadster, Dartmouth, 1930.

Dartmouth portrait, spring 1932.

With Fritz von Rehlingen in Europe, 1934–35.

With my parents, Mary Cord and Charles Alfred Odegaard, ca. 1940.

Betty Ketchum Odegaard, ca. 1941.

As a Navy lieutenant, 1942.

With Betty and our new daughter, Mary Ann,
August 1943, Urbana.

At the American Council of Learned Societies, Washington, D.C.

Fishing with Don Anderson, ca. 1958, Edmonds, Washington.
Photo by James O. Sneddon, Office of Public Information,
University of Washington.

◄ *As President of the University of Washington.*
Photo by James O. Sneddon, Office of Information Services,
University of Washington.

Presenting the University of Washington seal and history to
President John F. Kennedy on November 16, 1961,
at the University's centennial celebration. Office of Information
Services, University of Washington.

With Mary Ann at the 1961 Christmas Ball.

Betty, ca. 1963. Photo by James O. Sneddon,
Office of Public Information, University of Washington.

With the Odegaard Undergraduate Library in the background, 1973.
Photo by James O. Sneddon, Office of Information Services,
University of Washington.

UW Board of Regents, September 28, 1973; left to right:
Robert Flennaugh, Mort Frayn, Jack Neupert, Charles E. Odegaard,
Robert Philip, George Powell, Harold Shefelman, and James Ellis.
Photo by John A. Moore, Office of Information Services,
University of Washington.

"CEO Day," a campus-wide retirement party, was held May 11, 1973.

Mary Ann and Charlie Quarton with bust of Grandpa Charles, 1979.

Meeting Queen Elizabeth, March 1983.

With my grandchildren in Oakland, California, Christmas 1985.

OVERLEAF

On Bainbridge Island, Washington, ca. 1988.

In front of my portrait in the Odegaard Undergraduate Library, ca. 1990.

walking behind me toward the door. They might have heard what I was saying. Then Herr Sammiller asked me in a kindly manner in German if I knew about "the German Look." When I answered in the negative, he demonstrated by looking backward over his left and right shoulders.

One Saturday early in my stay, the Sammillers took Fritz and me in their Mercedes sedan southward toward the mountains and Ettal, the site of a monastery founded in the early fourteenth century, which still housed a boys' school that Fritz attended. From there we continued to Partenkirchen, where Frau Sammiller's family had long owned a beautiful villa. The hill behind it leads up to Zugspitze, Germany's highest mountain. The ski center of Garmisch is close to Partenkirchen.

On Sunday we returned to Munich by way of the famous Oberammergau. Back in Munich for several weeks, I took advantage of cheap seats for a number of operas, orchestral performances, and magnificent masses. On a lighter note I visited cafés and beer halls with Fritz and some of his friends. I also settled by day in the nearby University of Munich library to read from a number of interesting medieval chronicles. My Munich experience, while shorter, was as enriching culturally and historically as my Paris experience, in each case aided by my hosting families, the Tramonds and the Sammillers.

Travel in the French Provinces

I HAD PREPARED myself for travel in France by some intense reading at Harvard on the development of Romanesque and Gothic architecture. By short trips northward from Paris I had seen a number of major monuments. For my return trip from Munich to Paris, I planned a zigzag route through central and southern France to enable me to see medieval churches, monasteries, castles, walled cities, and towns. On April 28, 1935, I left Munich by train for Strasbourg, where I was able to purchase for 255 francs a half-fare ticket on the French railways, which, given the length of my ultimate itinerary, would turn out to be a good bargain. A number of towns along the way were centers of the local governmental departments into which France is divided, and they possess local archival collections often dating back to the Middle Ages. In some of them I found interesting historical documents, but the most rewarding findings for me were the old buildings in towns and villages which dated back to the Middle Ages and in some cases to the Roman occupation of Gaul. With innumerable stops in between, I passed by rail from Strasbourg south and westward through Langres, Dijon, and Cluny to Macon. Then I made a major jump south to the walled city of Carcassonne. After a short but wonderful interlude there financed by a Christmas gift from my parents, I went north and east to Nîmes, Arles, Avignon, and Le Puy. A chugging train ride over the *massif central* of France took me northwest to Bourges, Blois, and Angers. Then, by way of Le Mans and Chartres, I returned to Paris on May 28, 1935.

I was warmly welcomed by Mme. Tramond, but found the apartment reorganized and being repainted. Bill Jones had returned from Vienna previously and he was ensconced in my former room. I was placed in what had been the room for Michel and Martial, and yet another room was occupied by a student from Ireland. A bit of news was that Harvard University seemed likely to buy Professor Tramond's remarkable collection of history books, which Myron Gilmore and I had inventoried after his death.

I also learned that French friends from our Atlantic crossing had offered to take Myron and me on a three-day trip in their automobile through the northeastern corner of Normandy above the Seine River, the picturesque Pays de Caux. Myron and I then were driven to Rouen, from which we returned to Paris. The two of us also spent a weekend in Chartres with our mentor from Harvard, Charles Taylor. Our visit coincided with a splendid, colorful mass in that gorgeous structure illuminated by its stained glass. Following that weekend, I spent six days visiting a magnificent collection of eight cathedrals north of Paris.

On June 21, Mme. Tramond, her sister, and brother-in-law accompanied me to the train station, where I said farewell to the lovely Tramond family and headed for Normandy and the incredible monastic buildings of Mont Saint Michel. They tower above a rocky pinnacle in the middle of a very large bay. Fortunately for me, my companion on this trip to Normandy was Arthur Odell, an architecture student from North Carolina who was destined to become a very distinguished architect. We then visited other churches and castles in Normandy. Among the latter were numerous relics of the Norman dukes, including the Duke William who invaded England in 1066 and initiated the Norman line of kings of England. I spent my final day on the continent of Europe, leaving Arthur and taking the ferry to England on June 29, 1935.

A Brief Postlude in England

ON LANDING IN ENGLAND I proceeded directly to Oxford, where I spent a week with my Dartmouth classmate and Rhodes scholar Howland Sargeant, who served for me as a guide through the college and university grounds and their environs. I then joined Myron Gilmore in a rooming house in London and began to savor living in that metropolis. By July 16, I had encountered in the mail room at American Express Charles Ryan, my Dartmouth classmate and roommate for two years at Harvard. He and a fellow Harvard law student had planned a two-week auto trip through southern and western England with stops at many important and interesting sites. I was asked to join them. By the end of a week's sightseeing we had reached an attractive inn in Wells, where I felt the beginning of a heavy cold. Hoping that a rest would be helpful, I decided to stay a few days in Wells, and urged Ryan and his friend to continue their travel to the west.

I remained for several days in Wells and then was able to get a room in London in Miss Hibbs's boarding house, where Myron and I had stayed previously. My infection continued and fortunately Myron returned to the same boarding house. I had a return ticket to New York on the *Ilsenstein*, and would have to take a ferry across the Channel to board the ship at Le Havre, presumably on July 30. Myron, concerned about my health, was determined to find an easier alternative. He took my ticket and somehow exchanged it at virtually no cost for a third-class ticket on the *Europa*, more easily available to me in England by the boat train to Southampton. Once aboard the *Europa*, a ship's physician came to my cabin, gave me medications, placed cold packs on my chest, and kept me in my bunk for four days. Only on the fifth day did I get up and about. On the sixth day, I left the ship in New York to begin a bus ride to my family home in Evanston, after completing a wonderfully informative academic year in Europe.

That traveling fellowship was far more than a touristic experience for me as an incipient historian. At Dartmouth and Harvard I had read about the Middle Ages. But during the fellowship I had seen many surviving monuments of life as it was lived in cities, towns, and countryside during the Middle Ages. I had gained a sense of the reality of the past and how it conditions the present. This awareness was reenforced by my immediate contact with handwritten parchment documents, records written by living people whose words reached me directly, though they were long dead.

This experience convinced me of the importance of history in learning how our human past still affects our lives. It can help us sharpen our perspective on what we may want to change and what we may choose to keep. During that year in Europe the history of the Middle Ages became a real part of my cultural background, deserving of study for its consequences of good or evil in my own time.

Building a
Doctoral Thesis
at Harvard,
1935–1937

FORTUNATELY FOR ME, I COULD RETURN TO BOSTON
and Harvard from my travels in Europe with a waiver of tuition for
the academic year 1935–36 and a $1,000 salary for an assistantship
in the general European History course for Radcliffe's first-year
women students. This course was supervised in the first semester
by Professor Charles Taylor and in the second by Professor Sidney
Fay, both of the Harvard faculty. While they provided the lectures
throughout the year, we assistants supervised weekly discussion
sessions and read and graded student examinations. For a $150 fee
I also read and graded examinations of Harvard students enrolled
in Professor McIlwain's course on English constitutional history. A
similar arrangement provided financial support for my last year at
Harvard, 1936–37.

Returning to Cambridge in September 1935, I was fortunate to
find a room in dear old Nora Murphy's rooming house several
blocks north of the Harvard Yard. She provided a light breakfast
for her four or five tenants, but we were dependent for our other

meals on restaurants in the Harvard Square area. Most of my free time in 1935–36 was spent in my cubicle in the Widener Library.

A radical change in my way of living came in the fall of 1936, probably as a consequence of my learning the previous fall that Harvard had an endowment that could support a German graduate student for a year's study. I obtained information and sent it to Fritz von Rehlingen, the older son of the Sammiller family in Munich. He submitted an application and was awarded the grant for 1936–37.

I drove to New York in a used Chrysler sedan to meet him as his ship docked. We proceeded directly to my family's home in Chicago, and were joined there by a Dartmouth classmate from New Orleans. We began a circle auto tour from Chicago through the Northwest, south along the Pacific Coast to San Diego, then east to New Orleans and north back to Chicago. Finally in September we left for Cambridge to begin the fall term at Harvard. Fritz and I went directly to the two-person suite assigned us in Dunster House, thanks, I am sure, to friendly faculty intervention on our behalf, the specifics of which I have never known.

This direct exposure to the relatively new Harvard House system gave Fritz and me enriched social and educational experiences beyond any we could find living in the rooming houses and apartments of Cambridge. The Harvard House system had been introduced by President Lowell a few years earlier primarily to expose Harvard undergraduates to a more informal intellectual contact with members of the Harvard faculty. Each professorial master of a house lived within the House structure in a home for his family where students might be invited for an occasional tea or luncheon.

In addition, a number of tutors from different disciplines were assigned to houses with offices in which they could meet students informally. A few might have their own living suites within the house. It was not uncommon to see distinguished Harvard senior faculty members affiliated with a particular house lunching with undergraduate students in the dining hall. Speakers were invited with some regularity to give talks in the evening followed by discussion with house members. As a graduate student resident in Dunster House, my own intellectual interests were nourished by casual conversation at luncheon or dinner with professors from a number of disciplines.

The Harvard House system even encouraged intellectual interchange among the faculty who were affiliated with a particular house to serve as tutors to its diverse undergraduate population. The system opened up the possibility of an occasional dinner featuring a speaker, but more often a smaller meeting occurred after dinner at which a speaker would make a presentation followed by discussion within the group. I was invited to attend such sessions, not only in Dunster House but in other houses through acquaintance with faculty members associated with them.

I remember one such session when Felix Frankfurter, then a Harvard professor of law but rumored to be a likely candidate for Supreme Court justice, presented as speaker an old friend and lawyer colleague, Heinrich Brüning. The latter was the recently deposed and last legally elected chancellor of Germany who had found asylum in the United States when Hitler seized the government. In lawyer-like fashion, Brüning told us that the German constitution did contain an emergency provision he could have invoked in an effort to block Hitler, but which seemed to him, as a constitutional lawyer, itself to be destructive of democratic government. In view of the obviously tyrannical nature of Hitler's Nazi government, Brüning could only regret his decision. His was certainly one of the most poignant speeches I have ever heard, and an example of opportunities made possible for Harvard undergraduate and graduate students as well as faculty by the initiation of the House system.

Such experiences led me later to campaign as a dean at the University of Michigan for a place to have a coffeepot in academic departments in order to spur faculty-student conversation. As president at the University of Washington I insisted that in constructing new buildings for academic departments each discipline be provided with space for coffee and conversation between students and faculty. In already established academic buildings we tried to eke out such spaces. Similarly, student residence halls should include generous meeting spaces for students and also faculty members. It is a pity that many universities do not have funds to make student housing a planned segment of the joint educational experience between students and faculty.

In Pursuit of a Thesis and a Ph.D.

AT THE TIME of my departure for Europe in September 1934, I had focused on a particular problem, the nature of the relationship and obligations of the bishops to the king of France, the determination of what was meant by the frequent reference to them as his *fideles*, his faithful. I had used my opportunities in Europe to study and collect texts from relevant archival documents and manuscripts primarily from the twelfth and thirteenth centuries.

Back at Harvard and immersed in the books on the Middle Ages in Widener Library, I became more and more troubled about the nature of the obligations of the bishops to the king, about the implications of oaths of fidelity and of vassalage. Curiosity led me backward in time to choose my thesis topic, "*Vassi* and *Fideles* in the Ninth Century." My thesis was accepted for the Ph.D. degree in 1937, and, with slight revisions, was published in 1945 by the Harvard University Press in the Harvard Historical Monographs series under the title *Vassi and Fideles in the Carolingian Empire*. The delay in publication was caused by a combination of fiscal shortages at the Press and my four years of service in the U.S. Navy from 1942 to 1946 in World War II.

During my archival searches in Europe I had concentrated on evidence from the twelfth and thirteenth centuries. Further study at Harvard prompted me to shift my focus to an earlier period, as explained in the Preface to the published version of my thesis:

The subject of this study may at first glance strike the reader as remarkably confined, for the historian interested in the political institutions of the earlier Middle Ages is accustomed to treatises which travel in seven-league boots such as those of Waitz, Brunner, and Fustel de Coulanges. Accordingly, the reader might suppose that the material presented here would be a heavy load of minutiae the general sense of which could be found already in the more expansive works. The genesis of this study, however, belies any such assumption, for its roots lie far afield. It was certainly not the end in view when I began research upon the political status of the French bishops in the twelfth and thirteenth centuries. It is none the less a product of investigations begun in this later field, for I found certain difficulties in the existing treatises which prevented an immediate solution to my original problem until the "background" was cleared. This itself has proved to be no easy task.

The "static quality" of the Middle Ages is a concept which no medievalist is now likely to accept, yet not infrequently there has been written sober medieval history which assumes, perhaps unconsciously, relatively unchanging conditions. Such an assumption underlies much lumping together of texts from widely different times and places and the application of the same terms and ideas to very different settings. It is important not to overlook the possible changes in terms within fairly restricted periods, changes such as those forcefully attested by a monk of Saint Père de Chartres named Paul who, living in the eleventh century, "speaks of a collection of charters, the most ancient of which dated from the ninth century: 'What changes! The rolls preserved in the archives of our abbey show that the peasants of that time lived under customs which those of today know no longer; even the words which they used are not those of the present day.' And further on: 'I have found the names of places, persons, and things changed since that time to such a degree that not only have they disappeared, but it is no longer possible to identify them; far from having preserved them, men do not even know them.'"

I then explained that I had confined my study to a relatively restricted period extending from 751 to 888, not on caprice but because this period was the first to provide historians with adequate material for the study of *vassi*, and it also had a certain intrinsic unity which permits the materials from it to be grouped together for study of its political institutions. It was both preceded and followed by a period of weakness on the part of the monarchy and by the disorganization of political life. But within this period the monarchy was strong enough to make itself felt at least in a measure by all men. I concluded that Carolingian material should be considered on its own merits as the best evidence for Carolingian conditions.

It was this evidence which became the basis for the thesis I presented to my mentor, Professor Charles Holt Taylor, a taskmaster who—I came to believe—was probably harder on himself than on his students. It must have been an awesome responsibility for him to follow in the footsteps of Charles Homer Haskins, to be sure that one had found the last bit of evidence and really had in hand the solution to the mystery of the past. More times than once he sent me back to the sources for more evidence.

Finally, one day I entered his office, typically cluttered with books not only on shelves but on all chairs other than the one on which he was seated at his desk. I took the books off one of the chairs and placed them on the floor, and set the chair where I could face him. I then told him that I had followed the various leads he had given me, some productive and some not, and that I wondered if it was not time to present the thesis, for better or for worse, to the doctoral committee. He agreed that it was. I reacted to his affirmative response with both relief and enormous gratitude to him as a mentor. He had acquired a tremendous fund of knowledge which he tried to inculcate in his students through his lectures and his insistence on an exhaustive search for evidence to support one's propositions. After I had undergone his scrutiny, the examination by the doctoral committee seemed almost relaxing.

Curricular Desserts

DURING THOSE TWO YEARS at harvard from 1935 to 1937, most of my time was spent reading texts and histories about Western Europe from the sixth to the thirteenth centuries. I did, however, take advantage of the opportunity to audit some excellent lectures in addition to those required for my assistantship in the Radcliffe version of History 1, the series delivered by Professors Taylor and Fay. I remember William Scott Ferguson lecturing on the ancient Greeks, Alfred North Whitehead on Greek philosophy, George La-Piana on medieval Italy, Samuel Eliot Morison on colonial America, and Arthur Schlesinger, Sr., on the building of the American Republic. In addition to the casual acquaintanceship resulting from my presence at these lectures, I had the good fortune to be invited to participate in the Schlesingers' Sunday afternoon "at home" receptions, and the Whiteheads' Sunday evening receptions. I could not have had a better introduction to the charms of academic life than that provided me by the faculty members I encountered first as an undergraduate at Dartmouth, and then as a graduate student at Harvard.

A Ph.D. and Its Accouterments

BY LATE APRIL 1937, I had accumulated a range of seminars and courses with grades sufficient for the Department of History to waive the general examination for the doctorate, and I had completed an oral examination and a doctoral thesis acceptable to the final committee for the Ph.D. degree. I was beginning to consider the economies available to me through an early departure from Cambridge for my parents' home in Illinois when I received a letter dated May 5, 1937, from Dr. Chase, Dean of the Harvard Graduate School, asking if I would be willing to serve at the commencement exercises, June 24, as marshal for the doctor's degree candidates. This responsibility would entail my remaining in Cambridge for most of June.

I telephoned my parents in Illinois to inform them of this new development. My father told me that his business was finally on a steady upswing, that he and my mother would like to come to Harvard to witness the event, and that rather than renting the necessary doctoral hat and gown, I should buy a very good quality version, the cost of which would be covered by my parents. They were thus present for the commencement ceremony, and that academic costume has survived being worn by me on innumerable other occasions at dozens of universities.

The commencement of 1937 was a colorful and stately affair. The graduating students formed two columns, one each on the outer edges of the walk extending through the middle of the Harvard Yard. Carrying a black rod with a silver top, I stood at the head of the Ph.D. candidates about twenty feet from the statue of John Harvard seated in front of University Hall. Following the Ph.D. candidates came the higher professional degree candidates, then the masters' candidates, and finally the baccalaureate candidates.

The platform party entered between the lines of the baccalaureate candidates, and marched toward those expecting to receive higher degrees. At the head of the platform party was the Sheriff of Middlesex County dressed in his colonial costume presumably to maintain order. Then came the members of the Board of Overseers in top hats and tails, followed similarly by the small number of members of the Harvard Corporation. Next came the President of Harvard University, wearing a somber black antique academic gown. Following him came the distinguished individuals who were to receive honorary degrees, each of whom was accompanied by an escort in the person of an eminent member of the Harvard faculty. Then followed a delegation from the Harvard faculty in their academic gowns.

As the last of these individuals passed me, I raised my rod as a symbol for the two lines of graduates to merge and follow the platform party to a quadrangle courtyard on the east side of Harvard Yard. After the platform party and all the degree candidates had taken their assigned seats, the commencement proceedings began. The one bit of memory I retain from that event is that the phrase used by the President at the moment of official awarding of the Ph.D. degree was that we awardees were "admitted to the company of educated men." I hope I am correct. Remember that the event I described occurred in the era of 1937! The ceremony ended my official connection with Harvard University, but left me with a lifelong gratitude to many Harvard teachers and friends and a confirmed desire to have a career in academe in which I might find a way to give back to students the thrills of new discoveries and enlarged understandings such as I had received from my teachers at Dartmouth and Harvard.

A Neophyte
at the University
of Illinois,
1937–1941

AS A NEW PH.D. IN THE SUMMER OF 1937, I COULD NOT
avoid a measure of apprehension in seeking employment as a
teacher at an American university or college. While the downward
plunge of the Great Depression had finally leveled off, no clear com-
pensating upsurge in funding new hiring at universities had become evident. I knew that some members of the Harvard faculty
were engaged in correspondence with faculty at other academic institutions concerning the availability of openings for recent Harvard Ph.D. graduates, and that my name was among those being
presented.

By the early summer of 1937, I learned that I was under consideration for an instructorship, possibly at $1,800 for the academic
year, in history at the University of Illinois at Urbana-Champaign.
The History Department expressed the hope that it might be able to
increase the salary. By early August I received a contract for $2,000
for the academic year 1937–38. For this and other reasons, as will
soon be evident, I think that I was indeed fortunate to have the
appointment.

The campus of the University of Illinois is roughly a large rectangle, a half-mile wide east and west, and a couple of miles long north and south. In the 1930s, academic buildings occupied the northern portion of the rectangle, while recreational facilities for students and then the university's own farmland and agricultural research facilities covered a great expanse to the south. On the east side of the campus lies Urbana, then primarily a residential town consisting mostly of single-family houses with a few apartment buildings and a small commercial district. West of the campus lay the then burgeoning city of Champaign, a growing commercial distribution center with some light industry. It also included a railroad station on the Illinois Central Railroad, a solid corps of mansions of the Victorian era and later, and, on its western fringes, an expanding area of new upscale housing adjoining the golf club.

In the thirties, housing in Urbana was more attuned to the pace and finances of the faculty than what one could find in Champaign. It was in a professional home in Urbana several blocks from the campus, surrounded by other homes of senior faculty, that I was able to rent a small room in early September 1937. For the first time in over five years I had enough discretionary income to afford something other than the junk furniture that had surrounded me while a student at Harvard.

I therefore bought for my new quarters a mahogany kneehole desk with matching armchair, an overstuffed reading chair and chairside table, a standing brass lamp, and a handsome eighteenth-century style mahogany highboy. I made that room slightly more than full with a twin bed and mattress equipped with a fabric cover and pillows which converted the bed by day into something like a settee. From the fall of 1937 to the late spring of 1941, I occupied accommodations in three pleasant professional homes in that neighborhood. The second was a large wood-paneled room, and the third a comfortable two-room suite.

The university itself had no faculty club, but there was a private Women's University Club, a rather large structure a block from the campus with rooms on the upper floors that could be rented by women faculty and staff. Dining facilities for the members were also available. A block away was a similarly independent but less commodious Men's University Club, which by the time of my arrival, in September 1937, had suffered a relatively greater shrinkage in membership during the penury of the Depression. The Men's University Club had fewer rooms to rent and was feeding on a regular basis a small number of male faculty members. Since the homes of many faculty members in Urbana were within easy walking distance of campus, for reasons of economy many faculty men had developed the practice of going home for lunch as well as dinner. The patronage of the Men's Club for lunch or dinner had shrunk to about a dozen faculty old-timers, bachelors or widowers.

It was into this coterie of old-timers in the Men's Club that there was injected in September 1937 a flock of some twenty male instructors newly equipped with Ph.D.s. In the years immediately preceding my arrival the university's declining budget had prevented it from making new appointments at higher academic ranks. An unusually large number of graduate students had been pressed into duty as teaching assistants in undergraduate courses. The first new move upward in finances was used to replace teaching assistants in the fall of 1937 with a clutch of new full instructors with Ph.D. degrees. Illinois repeated this stratagem a year later. Such infusions of new talent clearly brought to the campus bright, well-educated men from a wide variety of disciplines.

These active and energetic male newcomers quickly developed the habit of eating lunch and dinner at the Men's University Club and made it a center of intellectual discussion and exchange as well as a pleasant place for social gatherings. As their acquaintance with earlier members of the Illinois faculty grew, more and more old-timers were enticed into participating in activities at the club. When an older member of the faculty was the recipient of an honor, or a younger one for that matter, some means of local recognition in a social gathering at the club would be arranged.

Over several years the club became an antidote to the omnipresent hazard of narrow confinement within discipline boundaries. In those days a high proportion of the faculty were men. Thus the Men's University Club provided a friendly meeting ground for the new younger faculty members, and the ensuing revival of club dining and activities by older faculty encouraged growing intellectual interchange among old and young alike. This had specific consequences for an assignment to me, as I shall note.

The History Department at Illinois, 1937–1939

AT THE TIME of my arrival in 1937, the History Department had a sizable student following in several courses that joined large lecture sessions with small discussion groups. For both American and modern European history there were clusters of able senior professors who attracted a substantial number of undergraduates to their lecture courses, which were usually accompanied by small discussion sessions led by junior faculty. I found myself in the first year assigned to duty in the large course on Modern European History supervised by Professor Paul Van Brunt Jones, a quixotic and amusing man. I listened to lectures by him and occasionally others, conducted discussion sections for the undergraduates, and read and graded their examinations.

I became similarly involved as an assistant in an intriguing course on the history of England since the sixteenth century taught by Professor Frederick Dietz, a very able scholar who combined a political analysis of the evolution of Great Britain and her empire with a social and economic perspective on the British people. Professor Dietz was also responsible for general oversight of students enrolled in graduate programs in the History Department before each had a particular thesis supervisor. My association with him in his undergraduate course led to his request that I participate with him in general interaction with these new graduate students, an experience that led me to more and more contact with Dean Robert Carmichael and his staff in the office of the Graduate School.

There was another fairly senior member of the History Department who, like Dr. Dietz, was to be a lifelong friend and adviser:

Professor Joseph Ward Swain, a well-educated historian and student of the classical world who nevertheless found himself constrained in the teaching of courses on the ancient world, at least in the 1930s, by a kind of monopoly exercised by the imperious chairman of the Classics Department, Professor William Abbott Oldfather. The latter was a scholar and bibliophile of the first rank who enticed groups of scholars from eminent eastern universities to come to Urbana, even in its hot and humid summers, to consult the great classical collection in the University of Illinois Library and to share in discourse with the Illinois classicists. Constrained in his options to deal with the history of the classical world itself, Ward Swain used his classical background to trace the impact of classical ideas and history on European culture in the Renaissance and subsequently. With his perspective on the inheritances from the classical past in later European cultures, a conversation with Ward Swain was always rewarding.

Strangely enough, from the beginning of my tenure I had a very friendly relationship with Professor Oldfather. Within the first month I was invited to Sunday dinner at the Urbana Golf Club by the Oldfathers. They remained friendly in a casual way. The subject matter never turned to discussion of the Greco-Roman inheritance in the Middle Ages.

Indeed by 1946, when I had graduate students interested in medieval history and who needed to develop proficiency in reading medieval Latin, I thought that some member of the Classics Department faculty might be interested in teaching medieval Latin. When I was a freshman at Dartmouth, my classics professor had even started a volunteer group to read a Latin chronicle of the First Crusade, but no interest in anything medieval was expressed by members of the Classics Department at Illinois, and I had little opportunity for intellectual interchange with them.

Professor Lawrence Larson had been for years the professor of medieval history at Illinois as well as the chairman of the History Department. He had been the person primarily involved in my appointment, but by the time I arrived in Urbana he was in full retirement, and unfortunately ill health led to his death within a year. As chairman he was succeeded by William Spence Robertson, a distinguished historian of Latin America, a very formal person in manner but with an underlying kindness. He and his wife proved to be gracious hosts. Periodically they invited the entire history faculty to their beautiful home for a delicious dinner followed by an evening of interesting word games that encouraged relaxed and friendly relationships. I found my colleagues, older and younger, to be a congenial group.

In that first year at Illinois my membership in the Men's University Club was the key to friendly discourse with fellow instructors and older faculty members from other departments. A rectangular table seating about eight persons continued for a time to be the domain of the old-guard senior professors. It was accompanied in the center of the dining room by a new round table seating about ten persons frequented by the young guard. With the advent of a second crop of young instructors in the fall of 1938 and an increased attendance in the club by older faculty, interaction among older and younger faculty increased.

While the top officers of the club continued to be senior members, I found myself chairman of the House Committee charged with scheduling various events in the clubhouse. Lectures by distinguished older faculty were often initiated by younger members. There was more and more mixing of contacts among older and younger generations at the tables in the dining room. This continued in subsequent years and seemed to me a stimulus to intellectual relationships within the faculty. The University Club was for me the wedge that opened up a rewarding association with faculty members diverse in age, rank, and subject interest.

By way of illustration, that club was the site for my first contact with a senior officer of the university who was to prove a great help to me and to my scholarship. A few days after my arrival in Urbana, Professor Dietz told me that he would like to introduce me to the Men's University Club by taking me there as his luncheon guest. As we approached the club on a pleasant sunny day there were several men sitting in rocking chairs on the entrance porch. Professor Dietz identified a particular elderly gentleman among them as Phineas L. Windsor, head of the University Library. He then approached Windsor and introduced me to him as a new instructor in the History Department. The old gentleman responded graciously and my host led me into the club and to the dining room.

It transpired that Dr. Dietz had to depart soon for an unexpected appointment and he left me to complete my meal alone. When I finished and stepped onto the porch, the librarian, seated alone, graciously pointed to a chair beside him and asked me to sit down and tell him about my background and schooling. I told him of my undergraduate experience at Dartmouth, my graduate years at Harvard, and my pursuit of the Ph.D. in medieval history. He then asked about my experience in the Widener Library. After I had described my cubicle in Widener in the midst of the collection on the Middle Ages, he praised that institution and then turned to me directly and said in a most sincere manner that he would appreciate it very much if I would survey the situation of the medieval collection at Illinois and report my conclusions to him.

I was immediately overwhelmed by a sense of responsibility to respond to what I construed to be a sincere request for an assessment of the Library's medieval collections. Accordingly I spent at least six months prowling through these holdings before I felt I could respond. I found that several well-qualified medieval historians had been at Illinois in the opening decades of the twentieth century. They may well have had some responsibility for the remarkable presence of the great collections in folio and quarto volumes devoted to medieval historical records which I had also seen at Widener.

It was evident that Professor Larson, my immediate predecessor as a medievalist, had watched carefully for acquisition of materials associated with Great Britain and Scandinavia but that some increased attention might be needed for acquisition of separate annals and cartularies often published in the last hundred years as a result of studies by doctoral candidates particularly in France, Germany, and Italy.

I was aware that European booksellers produced from time to time printed lists of available books containing transcriptions of medieval records and documents. I began checking these titles against holdings in the University Library. Mr. Windsor soon introduced me to a Miss Garver, a senior member of the library staff, who initiated the practice of having a staff member check such catalogues on arrival to mark any item already in the library's collection. She then sent me the catalogues so that I could designate any items that should be bought for the library.

As a wonderful by-product of these contacts, I soon acquired a small room in the University Library as my personal study. In it I could retain for reference some of the library's books, including those many cumbersome folio and quarto volumes that contain the sources for so much of medieval history. There they also remained available for scrutiny as needed by the library staff.

It was in this happy hideout that I labored to produce historical articles about the Middle Ages which finally appeared in print in the 1940s in *Speculum*. I had good reason to be grateful to a kind and great librarian for the assistance I received as a medievalist at Illinois. He provided me with easy access to a treasure house of recorded medieval ideas, thoughts, and perspectives that indeed were not totally irrelevant to presumptions found in students I was encountering in central Illinois.

A Summer Interlude in Middle Europe, 1938

I WAS EAGER to see the surviving monuments of the Middle Ages in central Europe and decided to devote the summer months of 1938 to travel there. After short stays with members of the Tramond family in Paris and then at their seventeenth-century home in Correze, I zigzagged across the middle of Germany with stops to see medieval monuments on the way to Dresden, a beautiful city soon to be devastated. I then took the train to Prague. The train stopped at the town on the German side of the Czech border and all persons were told to leave the train. When its departure was announced, I was the only one to board the train from the German station. The Nazi occupation of Austria had already occurred and the Czechs were very fearful for their future.

After several days in their beautiful but tense city, I went by train to Budapest where on the surface at least the Merry Widow culture seemed alive and well. The cafés were full of white-uniformed officers waltzing with beautifully gowned women to music provided by the café orchestra. No one in Budapest seemed to have a care in the world, except perhaps for an elderly genteel guide who escorted me through the Parliament building and gave me a fairly detailed description of the two houses, an aristocratic upper house of great landowners and an elective lower house. He referred to the then head of state, Admiral Horthy, as the Regent. When I asked the guide who would replace the Admiral in the event of his death, his reply terminated our conversation. It was: "That is a question which is not asked in Hungary."

I arrived by train in Vienna in time to find my hotel and immediately go to bed for the night. The following morning I headed to an office address I had received from my old friend, Howland Sargeant, a Dartmouth classmate and former Rhodes scholar I had seen in New York immediately before my departure for Europe. He had given me the address of a young English woman in Vienna and asked me to be helpful to her in any way I could.

I found the street easily and was walking toward her address when I saw ahead in the next block a solid line of people standing against the front of the buildings. As I approached the entrance to her building, I saw that the line of people continued up the stairs to the specific office address Sargeant had given me. It turned out to be the office of the Quaker relief agency established by British initiative to aid the battered Austrian population after the end of World War I. The people in line were Jews fearful of the Nazi threat to purge them, but hopeful that they might with the help of the

Quakers obtain from abroad some hard currency to buy an exit from German controlled areas.

For the two evenings before my departure for Munich I took Sargeant's friend to dinner, during which she told me about her conversations that day with fearful people desperately seeking to escape Nazi control. On one evening we were in the middle of our main course at a table in the garden adjoining the restaurant when my guest seemed to freeze and stopped eating. I whispered to her, asking if she wanted to leave and she nodded assent. As she reached the door to the interior part of the restaurant, she asked if I had noticed the tall blond man who had taken a seat at a table near the one we had just left. She identified him as the Nazi official then in charge of race purification in Austria.

The next day I left Vienna by train for Munich and a reunion with the Sammiller family. They were just as cordial to me as they had been before, and this time Fritz and I could reminisce about our circle tour of America's West in the summer of 1936 and our academic year together at Dunster House and Harvard. By some kind of unspoken consent we simply did not bring up the contemporary political situation in Europe, or American politics in regard to Europe. Near the end of my brief stay in Munich, however, Fritz's mother suggested that she drive Fritz and me for luncheon to a restaurant on Lake Chiemsee. She had telephoned for a reservation on the open terrace but a cold breeze began to blow. Fritz volunteered to go and request a table inside.

As Frau Sammiller and I slowly walked up toward the restaurant, she turned to me and said, "You see how we have changed." I think I responded with nothing more than a nod. I took her meaning to be that we do not talk about politics in Germany. I believed then that the family's politics would have been anti-Nazi. It was several years after the end of World War II before I could reestablish contact with Fritz. He told me that his younger brother had been a participant in the famous plot of a group of German Army officers to assassinate Hitler which was aborted at the last minute. The participants were tortured to death, and his brother would have been among them were it not that his army unit had suddenly been thrown into the mighty Russian offensive at Stalingrad. Fritz told me that he hoped his brother died more mercifully in battle than he would have facing the tortures administered to those in the plot against Hitler.

During my visit to Munich that summer, much was made of the dedication of a new museum, the Haus der Deutschen Kunst, which was intended to present pure art as approved by Hitler. This event coincided with an enormous pageant scheduled to proceed up the great boulevard, Ludwigstrasse, passing by the Royal Palace of the Bavarian kings and the Opera House, then turning toward the Isar River and passing by the new museum. The major streets were decorated with innumerable Nazi banners, and in many squares were great braziers, ten feet or more tall, filled with oil and ignited at night to provide a spooky illumination.

The culmination the next day was an enormous historical parade in appropriate costumes which must have been borrowed from all the opera houses of Germany, and which presented in succession leaders of three empires: the ancient Roman emperors with their legions of soldiers, then Charlemagne and a succession of Holy Roman Emperors with their mounted knights on horses from the Middle Ages and the Renaissance, and finally Hitler and his Third Reich represented by a mass of uniformed contemporary German Army soldiers accompanied by huge guns, tanks, and other forms of weaponry.

By the time I left Munich for my next planned stop, Berlin, I had become overwhelmed by an increasing sense of turmoil and of fear of the Nazi threat to peace in Europe—as I moved from uneasy Prague to fearful Vienna, to boastful and at the time threatening Munich, and then to Berlin. The strange thing is that I have never been able to resurrect memories of my several days in Berlin. I cannot recall even where I stayed. I must have seen some of the major monuments and great public buildings. Even when I visited the city years after World War II, when there still survived some monuments from prewar years, I could not recover memories of any of them from my first visit.

The one persistent memory I have had over the years of that first visit to Berlin is walking in a great expanse of green grass and plantings in the city's parks. This perhaps is not surprising, considering that walking in a park may have been the chief therapy available to me for my sense of distress about the mounting threat to the human condition to which I was being exposed.

My itinerary called for me to go from Berlin by train to Copenhagen. I felt a lightening of spirit as I crossed the border into Denmark and soon entered that beautiful Scandinavian city. I then crossed the strait to Sweden and went to Stockholm, where I met on the agreed-upon day another instructor in history at the University of Illinois, Robert Bone, who was to be my fellow traveler for the remainder of the trip home to Illinois. We made a quick trip to the island of Visby in the Baltic, a great center for trading by multinational merchants in the later Middle Ages and with a legacy still of churches and buildings from that era. We then proceeded by train to Oslo, Norway.

After a few days there we took the train north and west to Molde on the Atlantic coast, then proceeded southward by bus and ferries over beautiful land and fjords, passing along the way mountain ridges, forests, farms, and villages, finally reaching the famous port of Bergen. It still contains late medieval buildings associated with major trading operations throughout northern Europe. We proceeded by ship from Norway to England, and from there to New York and by train to Urbana and home for the fall semester in September 1938.

Learning to Teach

DURING MY YEAR in Europe in 1934–35 and my three months' visit in 1938, I had seen many surviving monuments of the ancient and medieval past: walled cities, castles, cathedrals, monasteries, churches, walled farmhouses, wood and stucco town houses. I had been acutely conscious of the continuing imprint of the material medieval historical past on present generations in Europe. Of course, there were no comparable monuments in central Illinois, nor in the United States, to attest to the impact of the Middle Ages on the students in Urbana, to whom I returned in the fall of 1938 with an increased zeal for teaching history, especially medieval history.

I had become fascinated by the story of the collapse of the Roman Empire in the West with the ensuing destruction and barbarism of the sixth and seventh centuries, and of the subsequent effort beginning in the Middle Ages to reconstruct through the melding of old survivals and new inventions a more civilized order in the modern Western world. This story contained two themes: the effort to create a more orderly, peaceable, and lawful society; and the effort to form an ideological and moral framework for a civilized society by reworking the intellectual and religious traditions derived from Roman and Judaeo-Christian sources.

In the select company in which I had lived at Harvard these problems seemed very real, and my year and a subsequent summer in Europe in the presence of so many physical survivals from medieval times made the heritage from the Middle Ages in our modern culture obvious. However, for many of my students at Illinois in the late thirties before quick travel to Europe by air was possible, the relevance of the European Middle Ages to their lives was not apparent, and I found that I had to win their interest. Photographs and slides could help with physical objects but not with ideas and attitudes.

I gradually learned to start my teaching about the Middle Ages not from the beginning, but by working backward. I remember the startled looks when in 1939, on the first day of my course in the intellectual and religious history of the Middle Ages, I asked the class if anyone could state for me a value assertion about life in which, at least for now, he or she believed, and which would guide his or her actions. In the face of their hesitation I assured them it was not my function to dictate what their values should be or to judge them, but to help them see more clearly what their values were and the relation between their values and those of others.

It was not long before a lively discussion ensued, embodying inevitably Catholic, Protestant, and Jewish perspectives reflecting the European origins of most students at that time. I then suggested that we could enlarge the range of discussion by seeing what our European ancestors—intelligent and interesting human beings exposed to somewhat different life circumstances—had said about such matters. Within two weeks the students were reading and criticizing Augustine's *Confessions* and *The City of God*. By the end of the course they had a clearer understanding of their own inheritance from the not-so-distant Middle Ages, of the sources of similarities and differences among themselves, and of their own special and individual selfhood.

Following this experience, students often commented on their greater knowledge of themselves and their greater understanding of others, with whom they might not agree but could now comprehend more readily. Experience in teaching such a course also helped me clarify for myself the importance of humanistic learning, of learning about oneself as well as the other fellow. This aspect of learning has not been adequately emphasized in our American educational institutions during my lifetime.

A Major Event: Marriage, 1941

IT WAS THE ESTABLISHED custom at the University of Illinois for the president and his wife to be at home in their residence and garden on a Sunday afternoon in the fall and in the spring to host a reception for members of the faculty and staff. In the fall of 1940, I was making my annual pilgrimage to the residence when, as I entered the president's study, I was struck by the sight of the erect figure of a handsome woman in a beautiful brown coat with matching brown hat trimmed with beaver fur, a stunning appearance. I could not resist walking up to her and introducing myself. She responded with her name, Betty Ketchum. I asked if her mother was Mrs. Milo Ketchum. This proved to be the case.

My friends the Colvins, whom I saw often, were near neighbors of Mrs. Ketchum's in an apartment building close to the campus, and I had a speaking acquaintance with her. That encounter led to a few dates with Betty to go to movies before my departure for the December holidays, which began with a skiing interlude with two men friends in the snowy area where Wisconsin adjoins Michigan. This expedition was followed by Christmas and New Year's Day with my parents in Evanston.

I found that I could not get back to Urbana fast enough. Betty and I soon began making plans for marriage in Chicago at a small but beautiful Gothic chapel close to the Oriental Institute of the University of Chicago. Betty's sister Martha was married to Nielson Debevoise, a faculty member of the Institute, and their home was to be the place for our reception after the wedding, April 12, 1941. My parents were delighted with Betty, and my father, who served as my best man, was determined to have me at the church on time. The outcome was that we arrived at the chapel so early we had to pass the time by viewing mummies in the exhibition hall of the nearby Oriental Institute.

After a weekend honeymoon at the Drake Hotel in Chicago, Betty and I returned to Urbana and to my two-room suite, but we immediately planned and began construction of a one-story house with a large living and dining area opening onto an open porch, a kitchen, two bedrooms, and a bath. It was attractive enough that our contractor was asked to duplicate the house for another person, but he declined to do so. Thanks to his efficiency, Betty and I were happily situated by the summer of 1941 in our home, and jointly involved in our academic life.

While I was essentially a first-generation academic, Betty had much deeper roots in academic institutions. Her mother, Esther Beatty, had a grandfather who, as a veteran of the Revolutionary War, had acquired a veteran's rights to good farmland in the southernmost part of Ohio. He became rich enough to send his son for a college degree to Ohio University at Athens. That son was subsequently able to "take his portion" and head west to look for good farmland that could be acquired cheaply. He wisely bought fertile landholdings near Newton, Iowa, and built a large Victorian home there. He took an interest in higher education and caused a building for a college to be built not far from his home, but before long the entire student population left to serve in the Civil War, and the college died.

He did send his daughter Esther, Betty's mother, to Iowa State University for a bachelor's degree, and then toward the end of the century to Columbia University for a master's degree in food sciences. Following completion of that degree, Esther Beatty was appointed a member of the faculty at the University of Illinois as the first assistant to Miss Bevier, the founder of the School of Home Economics. It was there that she was destined to meet and soon marry a young instructor in engineering, Milo Smith Ketchum.

Milo Ketchum, or Dean Ketchum as I became accustomed to hearing him referred to by other academics, was clearly an imposing figure at six feet four inches. Adept in determining the strengths of materials used in construction, he strove to improve their reliability. He published seven books on the strength of materials and their design uses for engineers. His status is reflected in the positions he held. He became Dean of the College of Engineering at the University of Colorado. During World War I, he brought into service the national powder plant in Nitro, West Virginia. After the war he returned to his post at Colorado. In the early 1920s he went to the University of Pennsylvania as chairman of Civil Engineering and then returned to the University of Illinois as dean of Engineering. It was while she lived with her family in Urbana that Betty received her own A.B. degree from the University of Illinois.

This is a quick sketch of the academic background of my companion for the almost forty years of our trajectory together in universities. She knew about them and their ways, and she believed in the benefits of life in universities for faculties, staffs, and students. She had grown up in a household where her father and mother used their home to welcome university faculty and their guests. At all stages in our career together in the university world, Betty was pleased to greet warmly guests in our home.

Following her death in 1980, I received a tremendous number of letters from persons of many ranks and relationships to the University of Washington expressing their appreciation for her kindness to them in the president's residence and other places. It was in response to this outpouring of appreciation for her warmth of hospitality that I initiated and continue to contribute to the Betty Odegaard Memorial Fund, an endowment whose income can be used toward expenses incurred for receptions at the president's residence for faculty, staff, students, and friends of the University of Washington.

A Curricular Initiative at Illinois

BY 1940, a group of senior faculty in Arts and Sciences at Illinois had become concerned about the curriculum presented to undergraduate students. At Illinois, as at most research-oriented universities, the research imperative had led to a great diversity of subject matters in a growing number of separated disciplines, and faculties were failing to give students an opportunity to gain from their college experience a more liberal or general education. In the 1930s the University of Chicago and Columbia University were known for their efforts to reform the undergraduate curriculum. Among the courses proposed at Illinois in 1940 by its reforming leaders was one focused on the history of Western European political thought and institutions. The underpinning for modern concepts of individual political freedom and democratic government lies substantially in Greco-Roman and medieval and modern European precedents. I had been studying that aspect of Western Europe's intellectual and political history and was pleased to be asked to provide the lectures for that course.

A Quadrennial
Interlude
in the Navy,
1942–1946

ON SUNDAY, DECEMBER 7, 1941, MY WIFE AND I WERE
listening to the national radio broadcast of the New York Philhar-
monic Orchestra when it was interrupted to announce that the
Japanese fleet had attacked Pearl Harbor and thus brought the
United States into the Second World War. The following day, I was
scheduled to lecture at 9 A.M. to the students in that recently established class on the liberal tradition, but I must have ignored my
notes on the morning of December 8, 1941.

That catastrophic national event abruptly changed the lives of
so many people, and led to a four-year interruption in my lifetime
trajectory in academic institutions. In the Navy, I was to have an
intense exposure to men of very different skills and capacities, men
from diverse social origins and classes who were engaged in de-
manding and dangerous duties under my command. This experience provided me with a residue of knowledge about humankind
which was to be of great utility to me in my later roles and responsibilities. In addition, much of my four years in the Navy was to be
spent either as a "student" in naval training courses or as an "in-

structor" teaching and supervising military personnel in training courses or work situations. Thus, while my years in the Navy were an interruption in my academic journey, my experiences in the Navy turned out to be relevant in a number of respects to my experiences in universities.

My observations in Germany in 1935 and again in 1938 had convinced me that Hitler and the Nazi movement were a dire threat to civilization and that sooner or later Hitler would have to be stopped. With the Japanese attack on Pearl Harbor it was clear that the time for me to enter the war against Hitler and his allies had come. On December 8, 1941, I wrote a letter to the headquarters of the Ninth Naval District at Great Lakes, Illinois, volunteering my service in the Navy.

By a letter dated March 23, 1942, the Navy notified me that, subject to my passing the physical examination, I was appointed Lieutenant (jg), D-V(S), that is, deck, volunteer, special services, to rank from March 5, 1942. On March 31, 1942, orders were issued for me to proceed on April 14 to Boston to report for duty on the morning of April 16, 1942, at the Naval Training School (Local Defense), South Boston. I have never forgotten to this day that first set of orders. At 0900 we were told to stand in a muster line, positioning ourselves in succession with the alphabet of our surname. We were then informed that the typewriters ordered for this Navy installation had not arrived and that none were available. Therefore, our first task would be to write twenty-five copies of our orders, which covered three closely typed pages. It was a nerve-wracking, hand-wearying experience. It served to solidify the group.

It turned out that there were two groups of officers assembled in Boston that day. One was associated with local defense—that is, net tenders, small sub chasers, harbor defenses. There was some touch of the sea, some prior experience on water, about the men in that group. Those of us who were not in the local defense group envied them their salty ways. But, as it turned out, the landlubbers were to see much more of the sea very quickly. We were referred to as the Armed Guard group. In the beginning none of us knew what "armed guard" meant. In the first days, the favorite theory among us was that we would be responsible for guarding munitions factories. Our egos suffered from that until, on the third day, we learned that we would be in charge of gun crews on merchant ships.

In retrospect, the Armed Guard group appeared to be a superior group of about seventy men ranging in age from about thirty to forty, a few somewhat older and a few somewhat younger. At thirty-one, I was among the junior in years. The youngest in the group was Ensign Maddox, twenty-nine, who was to die within a few months after spending forty days on a raft in the South Atlantic, only a few days before the several survivors still aboard the raft were rescued.

All members of our group were college educated men with a rather heavy professional stamp. There were lawyers, architects, college teachers, businessmen, and bond salesmen. In view of the duty to which they were to be assigned, it was presumed they needed to be men of stability, good judgment, and independence.

In our four weeks of classroom instruction in South Boston, we were taught about gunnery, much of it irrelevant to the actual equipment we would encounter in the armament on merchant ships. We were taught a lot about Navy regulations, much of it irrelevant to the circumstances we would meet on merchant vessels. We did get some lectures on the merchant marine.

The most colorful lecturer was a Commander Gainard, who as merchant master of the SS *City of Flint* had managed to escape German naval units by skillfully guiding his ship stealthily through Norwegian waters. At the time he was speaking to us, however, there was an air of mystery and bravado about him. He gave us a lot of bad advice about handling the merchant officers and crew, including the message "to shoot the bastards" if they failed to behave in a proper Navy way. A more dismal part of the curriculum was provided by a desiccated old Navy commander who dictated a text on international law to us for five days, and then on the sixth provided us with a set of questions we could pass with flying colors if we had memorized our lecture notes.

After four weeks in Boston, half of our Armed Guard group was ordered to report to Little Creek, Virginia, and the other half, including me, was sent to Chicago, to the Navy facility at the outer end of the large Municipal Pier on Lake Michigan. On the fringe of the pier there had been mounted a row of Mark IX, 4-inch naval guns, the principal gun for destroyers during World War I. We faced very little bookwork in Chicago. Our principal task was to train groups of enlisted men in handling ammunition and loading 4-inch dummy shells into these guns.

At the beginning of the fourth week in Chicago I found myself in the first group of six officers ordered for four days aboard the USS *Dover*, then the oldest commissioned ship in the Navy. The original plan called for each of us officers in succession to be in command of a gun crew of six enlisted men firing the gun at a towed target in the middle of Lake Michigan. Because of the shortage of ammunition, however, we each had a ration of only three shells. We were told that we would subsequently encounter as anti-aircraft guns the 20 mm Oerlikon; but we could practice firing only the 30 caliber machine guns then aboard the ship.

On the Atlantic, June 1942 to July 1943

ON JUNE 15, 1942, that first group of six officers including me was detached with orders to go to New Orleans. On June 17, I received orders to board the SS *Margaret Lykes* as commander of the Armed Guard. For years this ship had been in service in the Gulf and the Caribbean, and it was overrun with rats and cockroaches. Weighing about 4,000 tons, she had a maximum speed of 11 knots with the wind behind her.

The experience of the chief mate was instructive. His previous ship, with no Armed Guard and no armament aboard, had been sunk by shellfire from a German submarine lying on the surface. Placing armament and the Armed Guard crew aboard the *Margaret Lykes* increased the likelihood that a submarine would prefer to remain submerged to avoid the risk of a shot from a surface gun on our ship breaching its watertight integrity, thus forcing it to the surface. To attack submerged, the submarine would have to use one or more of its limited number of torpedoes, thus reducing somewhat its destructive effectiveness.

When I went aboard the ship on June 17, sailors were installing on the fantail a 4-inch gun, which was not a Mark IX but a Mark VII dating from 1898, a wobbly model which the warrant gunner in charge, who had twenty-five years of service in the Navy, had never seen before. The shoreside gunners also installed the bases for four antiaircraft Oerlikon guns, but left the guns themselves in their original packing.

It was on the evening of June 24, 1942, that I first found myself ordered to be the commanding officer on the SS *Margaret Lykes* of the Navy gun crew, which consisted of six apprentice seamen, one crewman 2nd class, and Morin, a coxswain with seven years' service in the Navy. The merchant captain and mates would handle the conning and navigation of the ship. The chief engineer and his associates and technicians would handle the ship's power plant and the technical equipment. My Navy crew and I would be responsible for the defense of the ship against military attack.

On June 27, 1942, we sailed from New Orleans toward Pilottown at the mouth of the southwest pass of the Mississippi River. At dawn the next day we headed west toward Lake Charles, Louisiana. By eight in the morning we were far enough into the Gulf to test fire the 4-inch gun. Imagine our reaction when we fired the gun and nothing happened. After firing the gun with the same shell in it eight times, we could only conclude that we had either a hangfire or a misfire. As I recalled it, the longest hangfire then on record in the Navy was twenty minutes. The standard doctrine was to wait thirty minutes.

Having decided that it was time to find out what had happened, I ordered the gun crew to go forward of the center deckhouse. The merchant crew had already evidenced their confidence in the Navy gun crew by placing themselves forward of the deckhouse. After the Navy sailors had started forward, Morin, the coxswain, turned toward me, saluted, and requested permission to remain to open the gun plug for me. Recognizing how cumbersome it would be for one person to open the plug and at the same time reach for the shell as it came out of the gun, I ordered him to open the plug for me, and felt a surge of great appreciation and respect for him. As the shell came out of the gun, I looked at the primer on the base of the shell. I had actually seen the dents on primers at the base of shells fired on Lake Michigan, and speculated that the dent here may not have been as deep.

We then turned to the four Oerlikon guns which my Navy crew and I had removed from their packing boxes and mounted on stands. We followed the instructions as carefully as we knew how and endeavored to test fire these guns, but had no success with any one of them. What a depressing beginning.

I then went back to the 4-inch gun and took out its firing pin assembly. I wondered whether the spring had lost some of its strength with the passing of the years, and therefore had not hit the firing pin with a sufficient thump. I had found the chief engineer aboard to be a friendly person, and he undertook to fashion an additional washer which we then slipped in behind the spring to increase its tension. By the time we had finished this task with our inadequate equipment we were too close to Lake Charles, our first destination, to be able to test fire the gun then. While the ship was being loaded with rice and beans for delivery subsequently to the hungry people of Puerto Rico, I searched for an expert on Oerlikon guns. I finally found on another ship a petty officer who had some experience with them. He showed us how to fully seat the gun on its stand and speculated that now the gun would fire.

On July 9 we sailed alone from Lake Charles going eastward along the Gulf shore. As soon as we were clear for test firing, we loaded the 4-inch, which had been named Betsy by the Navy sailors. She fired with a very satisfactory "boom." The four Oerlikons were then fired without a hitch. The Navy sailors' spirits soared, and the merchant crew were obviously more friendly to us. We had been plotting on the chart reports of sinkings, and they indicated the presence of German submarines in quite a few locations in the Gulf. We were sailing alone without any armed escort, since the Navy had available no ships to accompany us. Our orders were, at night as darkness fell, virtually to pull up on the beach.

Fortunately, the coast in the Gulf area is largely devoid of rocks. We heaved the lead until we were in roughly thirty feet of water when the captain ordered the anchor to be dropped. We took this situation seriously because that day we had passed close to the overturned hull of a ship. Just the keel showed barely above the surface with little waves breaking over it, making it look almost like a sandbar.

At dawn we continued on our eastward trek, with our destination that night again the southwest pass of the Mississippi River. Off and on during the day we had been seeing fishing boats and shrimp boats that had come out from the shore. In the late afternoon, as the sun was getting lower, there were patches of light and areas of darkness produced by heavy, squally, small rain clouds.

With my binoculars I made out an object that looked like it might be a shrimp boat. It was then lost in a dark patch. When next sighted it was farther up on our port quarter. I concluded that it was the conning tower of a submarine just awash, with the bow toward us. Again it disappeared. The trainer on the gun could not see the target, so I quickly took his place. Only the conning tower appeared next and I ordered the pointer to fire. He did so just as the periscope disappeared beneath the surface of the water. We saw no further trace of that submarine.

Within an hour as we approached the southwest pass to the river, we received from the signal tower a message, "Do you have any survivors aboard?" We had to answer in the negative. An hour or so before sighting the submarine we had passed through an area containing a lot of flotsam—crates that would hold vegetables and other bits and pieces of floating objects—which I had studied with my binoculars. I had seen nothing in the way of boats or evidence of people, though the flotsam obviously came from a ship that had been sunk. We had to reply "No." I soon learned that a

United Fruit boat had been torpedoed that afternoon, apparently with no survivors.

In the following days we proceeded alone, eastward and then southward along the Gulf coast, stopping at night within harbors until we reached an anchorage off Key West, Florida, which had been made safe against German submarines by surrounding it with a minefield. On July 13, I went to my first convoy meeting. We sailed that day, preceded by three small escort vessels, in a five ship convoy eastward from Key West toward Puerto Rico.

After discharging our cargo in San Juan, we proceeded to four small ports on Puerto Rico to fill the ship with sugar produced in fields nearby. We then joined a convoy at Mayagüez and headed again for the anchorage at Key West. There a much larger convoy was assembled to sail to New York. As we rounded the tip of Florida we could see another convoy five or six miles from us. We saw two of its ships as they were obviously hit by torpedoes, one after the other. Both ships sank within a few minutes. There was something very final about seeing ships go down in this way, disappearing beneath the surface of the sea.

Our convoy was ordered into emergency turns and left the scene as rapidly as possible. As we proceeded northward along the U.S. coastline we passed ample evidence of previous sinkings. In some cases just a portion of the mast or part of the ship would show above the surface of the sea. We had left Mayagüez on August 5 and arrived in New York on August 22, with three brief stops along the way.

That first exposure to an eight-man crew was a learning experience for me as well as for them. Morin, the coxswain, was in his late twenties. Kleczkowski was probably at least as old as Morin. The others were callow youths about twenty. I even wonder if one or two had actually reached eighteen. The seaman 2nd class, Kennedy, had been in the Navy only a few weeks longer than the others, so they were all vastly inexperienced and little accustomed to Navy discipline. They had to make mistakes in order to learn; there were episodes like returning late from liberty, or coming aboard with a bottle of beer, or getting drunk, and even falling asleep on watch. These led to extra hours of duty or loss of liberty.

Morin, the coxswain, was an excellent petty officer. He knew a lot more about the Navy than I did, and in his own way he was a good teacher. He put in long hours doing his best to train the sailors in their handling of equipment and to encourage their naval demeanor. He obviously had pride in his service with the Navy.

Before our departure from New Orleans I had obtained copies of Navy training manuals for enlisted ratings which I used in sessions with my sailors to make them aware of various petty officer roles to which they might aspire. This was a learning experience for me as well as for these mostly very young men as we set about learning the ways of ships and men at sea.

It was also inevitably a sobering experience for this relatively very young crew, for we began our service at sea at the most hazardous place to be at the time in the Battle of the Atlantic.

The *Margaret Lykes* reached New York on August 22, 1942, and I received orders on September 19 to be detached from that ship and report to the SS *El Coston*. I soon found out the probable cause for this sudden shift in assignment when I went aboard the *El Coston* and met the officer I was to replace. He was an ROTC graduate with a commission in the Navy and was in the first batch of officers to be assigned to Armed Guard duty, a circumstance he probably resented because of a desire to be on regular Navy ships. He launched into a litany of complaints about various men in his fifteen man crew, most of whom he had placed on restriction now that they were back in Boston. He had several men jailed in Iceland on their last trip, but then found that for lack of any way of replacing them, he had to take them back aboard to return to Boston. He warned me of difficulties that lay ahead for me. As I walked about, I saw that his own room was very untidy, the crew quarters were messy, the Navy gear aboard not well stowed. I concluded that the best thing to do was relieve him and get him off the ship fast.

After my predecessor had disappeared over the side, I mustered the fifteen man crew and gave them a rigorous personnel inspection. I would certainly not have known how to do this three months earlier, but had learned a good deal from watching Morin on my first ship. I then gave the men a speech on what I expected of them, saying that I started by assuming that they would deliver as good sailors. I announced that whatever restrictions they may have been under as to liberty were all waived, and that while we were in port I would set up two sections, with one section at liberty at a time.

I had two voyages to Iceland and back to Boston with that crew, and I had no disciplinary troubles except for the sad case of one sailor who had previously been aboard another ship in convoy which had been torpedoed and sunk. He had been picked out of the water by another ship in the convoy, and within twenty-four hours that ship was torpedoed and sunk. Again he had been rescued. He was then assigned to the *El Coston*. Although he did his work conscientiously, as much as possible while at sea he avoided going below deck. He persisted in sleeping topside in whatever sheltered area he could find in preference to using his bunk below decks. By the end of his return from Iceland to Boston he looked terribly haggard. He was taciturn, and it took some time before I was able to open him up for conversation. I finally talked to him about shore duty, but he begged me not to transfer him. A couple of days before the ship was scheduled to sail from Boston to New York, he failed to return from liberty. I asked the men to search the bars where they thought he might be. I was at the point of having to report him as absent from duty to the shore Navy authorities when a crew member found him and led him back to the ship. He returned in no way belligerent and gave every appearance of being contrite and eager to resume his duties. I thought I could handle the punishment aboard and did not turn him in. We sailed to New York on the inside passage, and again I found that he would not go below decks even though the weather had turned bitterly cold.

I concluded that he should definitely be assigned to shore duty. With little time available, I succeeded in having him transferred to the sick bay in New York, and a relief for him was sent aboard. I found out later that the medical officer who examined him had said that all he suffered from was a yellow streak down his back, and sent him back to sea. Meanwhile a citation for this sailor had arrived in New York, commending his very good conduct during the earlier torpedoings. What a hollow honor! I never was able to learn anything about his subsequent history.

The *El Coston* was then based at Boston, the gathering point for supplies for Iceland, and she began a series of voyages. I was destined to make two trips to Iceland and back to Boston aboard her, the first between October 1 and 31, and the second between November 15 and December 15, 1942. Her standard ration for Iceland was drums of aviation gasoline in number 1 hold, and 500 and 1,000 pound aerial bombs loaded in the bottoms of holds 2, 3, 4, and 5. These were topped off with miscellaneous supplies to support the U.S. troops in Iceland.

Since the eastbound North Atlantic convoys were organized to depart from the harbor of New York, the *El Coston*, fully loaded in Boston, would sail through the inside passage provided by the Cape Cod Canal and Long Island Sound to New York Harbor, there to join the other ships in the UK convoy. The standard practice was for the *El Coston* at sunset on the third day to increase her speed to 15 knots, pulling ahead of the convoy, and then on a zigzag course to head for Iceland. Each of the convoys we left at sunset on the third day to turn toward Iceland were attacked subsequently by German submarines.

We reached Reykjavik on the first voyage there as the land batteries were driving off a raid by German planes. For both return trips from Reykjavik to Boston the *El Coston* zigzagged at maximum speed and reached Boston without incident in seven days. In retrospect I think that those days aboard the *El Coston* were among the days of greatest continuous tension, the most arduous, and in a sense the most heroic of my war experience. There were ships being lost all around us. At each port we would find that old friends were gone.

On January 23, 1943, I received orders detaching me from the *El Coston* for reassignment to the USAT *Cristobal*, one of a number of ships under charter to the U.S. Army to carry Army garrison troops to locations abroad. She could carry up to 3,000 troops. The Army placed aboard its chartered transports an officer as troop commander with a couple of enlisted men assistants. It was their responsibility to deal with Army personnel aboard. My responsibility was for the defense of the ship. I had been promoted to the rank of Lieutenant USNR by March 1943 when the *Cristobal* sailed in a convoy of twenty-two ships escorted by the battleship USS *New York*, the cruiser USS *Brooklyn*, and nine destroyers.

On five days of the outbound voyage the escort vessels dropped depth charges or had radar contacts that indicated the presence of submarines, but no attack on the convoy itself occurred. Near Gibraltar those ships heading for Casablanca proceeded under American escort to their destination, whereas the *Cristobal* and the other ships entered the Mediterranean under British escort and proceeded to deliver their troops to Oran, Algeria.

For the return trip to New York the *Cristobal* was loaded with over a thousand Italian and 150 German prisoners of war. Apart from a brush with a German submarine astern of the convoy, there was no evidence of an effort to make an attack on the ships in the convoy.

The *Cristobal* with the same Navy gun crew aboard sailed on April 29, 1943, again from New York in a convoy of twenty-three ships, mostly transports, with an escort consisting of the USS *Texas* and nine destroyers. The *Cristobal* carried 3,000 American troops to Oran, who were destined to join the battle against Italy and Germany. In six days the convoy went through evasive maneuvers while depth charges were dropped on presumed submarine contacts, but it safely reached Oran on May 11.

About 1,200 German prisoners of war from Rommel's army in North Africa in the custody of a U.S. Army unit were taken aboard the *Cristobal*, which left Oran on May 19, 1943, in a convoy under the escort of two British aircraft carriers and eight destroyers or corvettes. There were six different sets of contacts with enemy submarines with the dropping of depth charges, but no ships were lost in the voyage to Gourock, Scotland. With her cargo of German prisoners the *Cristobal* was ordered to proceed up the narrow and twisting Clyde River with two tugs on her bow and two on her stern to a dock in Glasgow where the prisoners could walk ashore on a gangway.

The *Cristobal* returned quickly to Gourock, where it was loaded by lighters with British Army and Air Force troops headed for Algiers. The escort was provided by the HMS *Uganda* and thirteen British destroyers. There were ten episodes of contact with enemy submarines by the escorts with attendant depth charges, and in one case with gunfire from a destroyer, but the convoy itself was untouched and reached Algiers on June 27, 1943. As we approached the dock the *Cristobal* received a signal to unload her troops as rapidly as possible, and to load immediately to extreme capacity with British army personnel.

It was at this time that every effort was being made to move men and materials eastward along the African coast by roads and railroads to jumping-off places for the forthcoming invasion of Sicily and Italy. We never knew how many men we had aboard. Every bunk was filled and men were lying in the passageways and on the open deck when, fortunately, the weather was good and sleep was possible.

Under the escort of four British destroyers, the two ships sailed eastward on June 28 along the Algerian coast to Phillipville, which lies close to the border of Tunisia, arriving there and debarking our passengers immediately. On June 29 the two ships sailed with the three British destroyers as escorts to Gibraltar. Then three American destroyers provided the escort for the two transports and three other ships in a 16 knot convoy from Gibraltar to Casablanca. Again the *Cristobal* took aboard German prisoners and then found itself assigned to a convoy of some forty ships, mostly freighters, which could travel at a speed of 9.5 knots. The American escort consisted of eight destroyers and, for the first time in my experience, a small aircraft carrier, a so-called jeep carrier.

The convoy sailed on July 19, and made a dip far to the south below the equator, hoping to evade a German sub pack. The maneuver was not successful. For at least seven days the convoy was shadowed by enemy submarines. On eight occasions there were depth charges dropped by escorts around the convoy, and many emergency turns and evasive course changes were instituted during these days.

When we reached the dock in New York on July 21, 1943, I was the first ashore in search of a pay phone to telephone my wife in Urbana. I learned thereby that I had a lovely daughter, Mary Ann, born June 28, 1943. A few days later I was given orders detaching me from the *Cristobal*, granting me fifteen days leave, and ordering me to report to the Commandant of the 12th Naval District in San Francisco, California, for assignment to duty as Commanding Officer of Troops.

That leave was a blessing. It permitted me to stop in Urbana, on the way west to San Francisco, for a family reunion including wonderful days in which I met my new daughter.

Transports on the Pacific,
August 1943 to November 1944

THERE IS A STORY BEHIND my assignment to duty as commanding officer of troops. By the early part of 1943 the Navy had found itself, for its island-hopping campaigns in the central and south Pacific, in need of more ships than it had been able to obtain as commissioned ships, particularly to transport Navy, Marine, and Army troops to and from various destinations in the Pacific area. Therefore the Navy had to charter merchant ships that could also be equipped to serve as troop carriers. There were Armed Guard units aboard these ships, but their officers had been assigned no responsibilities toward the troops. When troops were placed aboard, the senior officer among them was designated as the commanding officer of troops and was responsible for their discipline and military management while aboard the vessel.

When these ships reached the island destination on the outward voyage, there was a great temptation for groups to take from the ship any items they thought might be useful to them in their new circumstances. There was little pressure from the commanding officer of troops, who would be leaving along with them, to stop this kind of stripping of a ship, which after all was headed back toward civilization. The result was that these merchant ships which had been used as troop carriers were often returning to San Francisco sufficiently stripped to warrant an unexpected stay in the yards for refurbishing.

The port director for San Francisco at that time was a man of remarkable energy and ability, Captain Milton Davis. It is my understanding that he was the one who decided that it would be necessary to place some naval officer aboard these ships chartered to the Navy with responsibility for the behavior of the troops aboard, to forestall this continuing depredation of the ships.

Seven Armed Guard officers from the Atlantic transports, including me, were given orders to duty as commanding officers of troops. We were to find ourselves again at the beginning of a new kind of duty. I would join the *Young America*, a C-2 hull good for about 14 knots maximum, a freighter recently converted for the carrying of troops. On September 2, 1943, the *Young America* sailed from San Francisco to Port Hueneme, California, where the ship was to take aboard Acorn 13, a Navy airfield unit, and also the 71st Construction Battalion (subsequently a highly decorated Seabee unit) for a total number of 69 officers and 1,565 men.

The *Young America* sailed alone from Port Hueneme on September 7, 1943, arriving September 19 at Pago Pago, Samoa, there to await an escort. We then sailed to the New Hebrides, stopping there to wait for unloading opportunities at our destination, Guadalcanal, which we reached on October 5. We began unloading by lighters, but finally were able to unload on the only dock which had been built on Guadalcanal.

On October 10, 1943, the *Young America* left Guadalcanal, arriving in Pearl Harbor on October 24. There the ship was placed under the command of the 5th Amphibious Force to be used along with a number of other chartered transports in the forthcoming invasion of the Gilbert Islands. A whole new chapter opened up as the Navy's crew of 5 officers and 50 enlisted was increased to 10 officers and 120 enlisted men to provide boat crews for LCVPs and LCMs placed aboard the ship for rapid unloading of men and materiel in the forward areas. The *Young America* was also destined to become a Commodore's ship for a Task Group, with the Commodore's staff of five officers under the command of Captain Paul P. Blackburn, a very able officer.

By November 14, 65 Army officers and 921 enlisted men of the Army had boarded the ship. They were part of the garrison force intended to occupy the island of Makin in the Gilberts after it had been taken by the Marine assault forces. The *Young America* and her convoy escorts left Pearl Harbor on December 15, 1943, and on D-day plus four, in the assault on Makin, the *Young America* entered the lagoon to begin unloading.

Our ship was thus a participant in the first invasion of Japanese-held islands in the central Pacific. Whereas General MacArthur was in command of operations in the south Pacific, Admiral Nimitz was in command of the central Pacific offensive, operating from his headquarters in Pearl Harbor. This first offensive had as its targets the islands of Makin and Tarawa in the Gilbert Islands. Makin was less heavily defended by a smaller Japanese garrison force and was quickly overcome. Tarawa had a much larger garrison force, and its defenders had erected just above the beaches a defensive wall constructed of coconut palm logs which proved to be unexpectedly capable of absorbing shellfire from Navy guns and therefore more durable under attack.

To add to the difficulty, the attack on Tarawa occurred coincidentally with an unusual phenomenon called a dodging tide. The outgoing tide, instead of running off at an even rate, dropped suddenly, and many of the small U.S. Marine landing craft on their dash to the shore suddenly found themselves beached within the range of machine gun fire from the Japanese log defenses and still far from contact with the defenders. The result was an immediate high casualty rate among the U.S. marines. The Navy learned from this experience to engage in subsequent invasions in far heavier shelling of beach installations by naval guns before launching troops ashore.

The *Young America* was the first ship to be piloted through the coral reef into the lagoon to unload the Army garrison troops and their supplies. Of the thirty hatchmen and winchmen upon whom the burden of 24-hour unloading into small boats depended, twenty-one had never touched a winch before boarding the ship. Two had actually had some experience. Four had three days' training, one had a day's training, and two had three hours of training. There were no petty officers among them, but there were some who showed real leadership.

The merchant crew, carefully respecting their rules as to hours, confined their attention largely to the maintenance of the gear, with the actual unloading left to the Navy sailors under my amateur direction. There was every reason to unload as rapidly as possible because the Navy Task Group located around Makin and Tarawa, with the help of fighters from its carriers, had to provide a screen against Japanese planes from the Marshall Islands. Only once did their bombers get through to fly over the Makin lagoon, where U.S. destroyers helped to drive them off without damage to the ships.

Since this was the first time the Navy had used chartered transports for amphibious landings, Admiral Turner, commander of the 5th Amphibious Force, sent his chief of staff, Captain Paul Theiss, and his staff gunnery officer, Commander John Taylor, aboard the *Young America* to observe the unloading procedures.

Captain Theiss, recognizing that it would be necessary to use merchant ships in these unusual situations, asked me to submit a special report of recommendations for this type of ship, by then designated an XAP. He himself wrote an extended memorandum critiquing the operation and recommending that on merchant-operated APs the commanding officer of troops should be a Lieutenant Commander whose prestige should be increased in order for him to deal adequately with superior officers to whom he must give instructions and even orders, as well as to the ship's company. Admiral Turner subsequently recommended to the Commander of the U.S. Pacific Fleet that there should be established a commander of naval detachment aboard XAPs.

The *Young America* sailed from Makin on November 29, 1943, reaching Honolulu on December 8. While still at sea I wrote a letter to the Commander of the 5th Amphibious Force requesting repairs and alterations to the *Young America*, a letter written in accordance with my instructions to submit requests to higher authority for changes I felt would improve the efficiency of the ship. I divided the requests into two parts, those useful for operation as a straight transport of XAP and those useful for amphibious operations. Upon arrival in Honolulu the commodore staff and the communications team were detached, and it was learned that the ship had been transferred from the 5th Amphibious Force to the Service Force, Pacific, with orders to sail the following day to San Francisco.

Upon my return to the port director's office in San Francisco I was told that the ship's captain had complained about me to the War Shipping Administration, and I was asked to write a report concerning our relations. On December 16, I submitted a report about the relations between the merchant marine personnel and Navy personnel aboard the ship, and appended a number of documents which illustrated incidents aboard ship. I concluded with the statement that on the recent operation Captains Paul Blackburn and Paul Theiss and Commander John Taylor had ample opportunity to see conditions aboard the *Young America* during the unloading in Makin, and that they had openly condemned to me the unsatisfactory state of the merchant marine aboard, placing the principal blame on the weakness of the master. Subsequently, Captain Blackburn and Commander Taylor both wrote letters in support of my performance of duty, and Admiral Turner of the 5th Amphibious Force wrote a letter to the Navy Department recommending my promotion to Lieutenant Commander on the basis of the reports he had received from his staff. By the time that was received the Port Director of San Francisco had already, on March 4, 1944, effected my spot promotion to Lieutenant Commander.

While the *Young America* was in San Francisco, the ship's captain was transferred and replaced by a new master who maintained somewhat more discipline in the merchant crew, but was a chilly character, obviously prejudiced against the Navy by his predecessor. The best we could maintain was a cold indifference to one another. The ship was ordered back to Pearl Harbor, returning there on December 30, 1943.

With the ship placed under the 5th Amphibious Force, Pacific Fleet, for the upcoming Marshall Islands invasion, I received orders on January 26, 1944, as Commander, Naval Detachment, to coordinate the activities of the various naval units on board, and through the master the activities of the merchant crew details and the naval details for all practical purposes. My contact was with the chief mate, with whom I had amicable relations.

The *Young America* was again designated as flagship for a task group under Captain Blackburn, who again came aboard with his staff. On January 28, 1944, we sailed in convoy toward the Marshall Islands. There were two primary targets in the invasion of these islands, Kwajalein and two small islands linked by a short bridge, Roi and Namur. The *Young America* was headed for the latter. Almost the entire surface of Roi was covered by the airfield proper, which the Japanese had built. Namur was used for the housing and service functions associated with the airstrip.

The *Young America* on the sixth day of the attack entered the lagoon and lay close to the two islands. The assault force, the 4th Marine Division, having captured the two islands, the *Young Amer-*

ica on February 5 was able to discharge its passengers, the 34 officers and 621 enlisted men who were to operate the airport. By February 1 the last of its cargo had been discharged, and 100 officers and 1,428 men of the 4th Marine Division, the assault troops, had come aboard the ship.

We were lying there waiting for other ships to be discharged when, during the night and early morning of February 12, Japanese bombers from Ponape succeeded in flying over Roi. Their first bomb landed on ammunition which had been stacked inevitably in the open on the surface of the runway. It produced a tremendous explosion, setting off many fires. Other bombs set fires among the gear spread along the beach. The bombers did not attack the ships in the harbor. The SS *Typhoon*, then empty of passengers, was designated the hospital ship to take aboard the many who were wounded on Roi. The *Young America* still had aboard a considerable store of medical supplies. The other ships were ordered to send their small boats to take these supplies to the *Typhoon*.

Later that day the *Young America* was ordered to sail. We took our Marines to a port on Maui on February 21 and on the following day went to Pearl Harbor. There we received orders on February 24 to sail without troops aboard to San Francisco, arriving there on March 3. It was there that I learned I was to be detached from the *Young America* and detained for a time on temporary duty in the port director's office as assistant in handling the chartered transport pool of officers and chartered transport problems. There also I learned that I had been spot promoted to Lieutenant Commander as of February 4, 1944.

In the port director's office between March and July 1944, I had the first opportunity to have a home life with my wife and my daughter, who had been born June 28, 1943, and whom I had seen only a few days in August 1943 and December 1943. I was scheduled to be assigned to duty aboard a new ship awaiting completion, the SS *Sea Runner*, when I learned on June 16 of the sudden death of my father in Florida. I was given emergency leave from June 17 to July 2.

I flew to Chicago, where I met my mother for my father's funeral there. Then I flew to Florida with her, helped her close her house in Lake Worth, and drove her in my father's car from Florida to California. On July 5, I was ordered to duty aboard the *Sea Runner*, which had been finished in the expectation that she would serve as an XAP.

We took from San Francisco to Pearl Harbor an Army regiment which was destined to be involved in the attack on the Philippines. The colonel of the regiment was an impressive man. I was very sorry to learn later that he was killed early in the attack on the Philippines. In Pearl Harbor the *Sea Runner* was again loaded with garrison personnel for the primary target in the Palau Islands, Peleliu and its airport. Colossal forces were gathered together around Pearl Harbor for this next operation. The *Sea Runner* left Pearl in a task group of about a dozen ships escorted by American destroyers. The American attack was still very much under way when we reached the major target area, Peleliu.

The *Sea Runner* and other ships with garrison forces aboard had been brought up close to Peleliu within a few days after the original attack, in the hope that the garrison forces could soon be sent ashore and the assault Marines taken aboard the transports. Given the expectation that the Japanese on Peleliu would soon be overwhelmed, the *Sea Runner* was ordered to remain close by the island even though it was impossible to anchor off Peleliu because of the extraordinary depth of the ocean there. For some days, therefore, the ship, staying close to the island, would slowly steam ahead to a point even with the north end of the island. The southward drift of the current would slowly take the ship southward until it lay off the southern tip of Peleliu.

On the top deck of the *Sea Runner*, using a signalman's 16 power glass, I could see the war going on over Bloody Nose Ridge. The Marines had secured the airstrip itself, but not the rocky ridge, hardly more than 300 to 400 yards from the edge of the airstrip. The Japanese had riddled the rock with caves; from time to time they would get to the entrance with machine guns and mortars which they would fire upon the Marines on the lower parts of the ridge, and even upon the airstrip with its planes and personnel. One could watch a number of U.S. planes take off from the airstrip, wheeling out over the sea, and then, coming back in the air virtually over the spot from which they had started on the ground, to make a run on the ridge itself, dropping from the first planes cans of napalm.

The last planes would drop charges which would set the napalm afire. With the long glass I could follow the slow movement of these rivers of fire as they made their way down the cracks and crevices of the ridge, hopefully getting into the caves of the Japanese. Meanwhile one could also see our own Marines scurrying along rocky ledges, also trying to rout the Japanese. One of our own hospital ships lay close to shore to receive our wounded, who were brought down from the ridge and placed aboard alligators—heavy-tracked vehicles that could crawl over the rocky heads of the corals and into the water, then to thrash their way to the gangway of the hospital ship.

Forty-five days after D-Day, the 1st Marine Division's responsibilities for the assault on Peleliu were taken over by an Army division. The *Sea Runner* returned to the area off the airfield on Peleliu, where we took aboard somewhat under 2,000 Marines, the remnant of about 4,00 men who had begun the assault on the island, the others being either the dead or the wounded who had been evacuated by plane or ship. The colonel in command of the Marine division had been killed on the first day of the landing on Peleliu. His successor, Lieutenant Colonel Boyd, was an excellent officer. The Navy crew aboard the *Sea Runner* had ample opportunity to observe the circumstances under which these Marine veterans of thirty months in the Pacific had just labored, and did everything they could to make the voyage back to the Marine base on the Russell Islands near Guadalcanal as pleasant as possible.

The trip from Peleliu to the Marine base passed without difficulty. We reached the debarking point about noon, and as the officers were leaving, Colonel Boyd told me that they were going to have a party that evening and would like me to join them. I expressed my regrets, saying I had to have all the ship's boats back aboard that evening because of our early departure the next morning. He assured me the Marines had a boat that could pick me up and get me back to the ship. I confessed to being flattered by the invitation to join their party. They were very hospitable and friendly. I spent a remarkable evening with these men who had been through so much and who were so appreciative of the very little that we had been able to do for them. A few days later, at Guadalcanal, we took aboard an Army regiment, a majority of whose members had been part of a Hawaiian National Guard Regiment established in the Honolulu area prior to World War II.

As we approached Hawaii we received orders to go directly into the harbor of Honolulu, to the main Matson dock. The minute we were inside the harbor area the *Sea Runner* was surrounded by all kinds of small craft, obviously carrying relatives of members of the two Hawaiian battalions there to greet their returning relatives, family members, and friends. The weather was beautiful and the troops aboard were all on the open deck. By some marvelous chance they broke into "Song of the Islands," and no Matson passenger liner had a more musical or more emotional landing than did the *Sea Runner* that day.

I was myself to have a surprise that same day. On the dock waiting for us to tie up I spotted Lieutenant Prince, a fellow officer in the Chartered Transport Pool. When he was able to come aboard, he greeted me with his orders to relieve me so that I could respond to orders to duty in San Francisco as officer in charge of the Chartered Transport Section in the Office of Port Director. I was detached from the *Sea Runner* on November 26, 1944, and fortunately the next day was able to board a ship departing for San Francisco. For the first time in my life in the Navy, I was on a ship at sea without any kind of command responsibility.

Duty Ashore in the Navy,
January 1945 to January 1946

MEANWHILE, MY OWN HISTORY as a historian was finally to catch up with me in July 1945. When World War II began, the Navy Department had found in its files very little in the way of a historical record of its activities during World War I which could provide much guidance for the conduct of World War II. By 1945, the Navy had concluded that an effort should be made to have the history of the activities of the Navy in World War II written for the future benefit of the Naval Service itself, but not intended as a public history. Various commands, accordingly, were ordered to appoint a historical officer.

The Commandant of the 12th Naval District, like other commandants, received orders to appoint a historical officer to be sought in the first instance among personnel within the district who might have such qualifications. My name came to light as one with a Ph.D. in history. I was granted twenty days leave, with orders to report for duty on July 23, 1945, as historical officer for the district. Thus ended my connection with chartered transports.

As it so happened, the atomic bombs were dropped on Japan only two weeks after I reported for duty as historical officer, and the war quickly came to an end. I was eligible under the point system for release from the Navy within a month of the end of the war; however, the regulations provided that any commanding officer could detain for four months beyond the eligible release date any officer whose retention was determined by him to be a military necessity. The Admiral of the 12th District invoked that provision in my case, making it impossible for me to return to the University of Illinois at the beginning of the fall semester of 1945.

There was the alternative that I might return for the second semester at the beginning of February 1946. I was in fact detached from duty in the Navy on January 4, 1946, with a terminal leave of one month, fourteen days, making my final day on military pay

February 16, 1946. I therefore had essentially the last five months of
1945 during which to work on the history of the 12th Naval District.
I left to my Navy successor an outline of the District Administrative History as I had developed it.

In mid-January 1946, I began driving my wife and daughter,
Betty and Mary Ann, back to Urbana and the University of Illinois
to take my role there as an associate professor of history.

An Epilogue for the Navy, 1942–1946

I AM SURE that my immersion in trying to write the history of the
activities and management of the 12th Naval District was a valuable
experience for me, really a learning experience. It forced me to continue to think about the management of men and the influence of
individual personalities; and administration, far from being a dry as
dust matter, became a very human affair, even in the large scale at-
tained by activities in the 12th Naval District during World War II.

After I ended my active duty in the Navy, I looked back over
those years of service and concluded that I had profited greatly in
terms of personal experience. The Navy did give me a peek at other
parts of the nation and the world which I had not previously seen.
It introduced me to New Orleans and San Francisco, and I saw parts
of the Gulf and Caribbean area. The Navy took me to Iceland, to
the north coast of Africa, and to Scotland, and then to Hawaii and
numerous islands in the south and central Pacific. Join the Navy
and see the world worked in my case.

In my Navy experience I was confronted repeatedly by unexpected situations from which there was no escape, and this at a time
when we lacked applicable books of instruction, when there were
few rules to guide one, when there were indeed legal rules sometimes in conflict with one another. I was the commanding officer of
Navy crews assigned to five ships in succession, the *Margaret Lykes*,
the *El Coston*, the *Cristobal*, the *Young America*, and the *Sea Runner*.
I began with a crew consisting of a coxswain and 7 seamen, and on

the last ship I had a Navy crew consisting of 12 officers and 150 seamen. On the last two ships I also had responsibilities as commanding officer of troops for supervising the troop organization for one to well over two thousand military personnel who were passengers aboard. A good bit of learning had to be by trial and error. It was probably fortunate that I moved from ship to ship, since it made it easier to leave one's errors behind and to approach each new assignment with some residue of success achieved in previous situations.

The war experience made me realize that there is a loneliness to life. There are inevitably things one has to face alone, and the experience forces one to look inside oneself in a more searching way. Against that inevitable sense of aloneness, one appreciates all the more those warmhearted moments in life that come from friendship. I am not surprised that men make mistakes in light of the greater awareness of the stresses life can bring to us. I came to expect less of mankind than I think I might have, and I appreciate more what men do. I treasure more those bridges that we are able to develop between one another. We are like separate ships that sail in convoy to our individually appointed ends, but as companions one to another.

A sense of responsibility for others set me to thinking a great deal about men and their diverse talents, their strengths and their weaknesses. Aboard a ship one has to live with deficient individuals; one cannot flunk a sailor overboard. There is an imperative to find at least something useful that a defective sailor can do. One might have to search one's brain to find a job for him; and at the same time there always seemed to be jobs for which better help was needed. This pressure led me to think a good deal about ways to elevate the ceiling over men. I discovered that, with guidance and help, men can usually learn to do more than one expected. I learned not to sell human talent short too quickly.

My experience in the Navy greatly expanded the scope of my contact with individuals from different levels of society and different cultural backgrounds. At one extreme were Filipovich and

Schreindl. Filipovich, a tall, powerfully built type, came from an eastern city slum. Schreindl had the stocky look of a boxer, complete with cauliflower ears, which, I heard from other sailors, were the result of repeated beatings he had taken, while he was growing up, from his father, a Nevada rancher. Both of them had originally escaped the hot breath of the draft into military service by voluntarily entering a merchant marine school for training as deck hands aboard merchant ships. To enter this program they had been required to sign up for the Navy Reserve, but they would not be called up for actual service in the Navy so long as they were studying to become merchant seamen.

They had proved to be incorrigibly bad actors while in the merchant marine school, and had been punished by being ejected from it and thus condemned to active duty in the Navy. They were first assigned to active duty as hatchmen and winchmen aboard the *Young America*. One can imagine the joy with which they entered naval service on this ship. They expressed their dissatisfaction by repeatedly quarreling and fighting with other sailors aboard and, helped by their addiction to hard liquor, by getting into constant difficulties ashore. They were the only sailors I never succeeded in getting under manageable control. When we reached Pearl Harbor, I was able to have them detached and replaced. I recommended to the shore authorities that they be assigned to nothing smaller than a battleship, and then only one to a ship.

Fortunately, there were men at the opposite extreme, such as Papolic, a very able signalman in his mid-twenties who had been raised in a New Jersey slum. He had come aboard just before we sailed on a tense voyage to Iceland, and I had not had much opportunity to learn about him. During the voyage he was seasick repeatedly. By the time we reached Iceland he looked miserable, but was always on duty and never complained.

Several nights after our arrival at the main dock in Reykjavik, I was spot checking the watches in the middle of the night. At one point I found myself standing beside Papolic while both of us contemplated a beautiful full moon — not one's favorite bit of scenery at that time and place, since the area was prone to German air raids, but beautiful nonetheless. Papolic broke the silence with what was clearly a quotation very apt for the occasion. I turned to him and asked, "Who said that?" He replied, "Marcus Aurelius." To my question, "Who was he?" he replied with a very quick and precise description. Then I asked him where he had learned about Marcus Aurelius, and he replied, "In a public library in a small town in Montana."

I gradually got the rest of the story. During the Depression he had been unable to get work and had signed up with the CCC, finding himself caring for forest lands in the Far West. On their one day of recreation each week the men were driven to a neighboring small town, and most of them headed for the bars on Main Street. But Papolic had discovered that the town had a small public library, and he went there to spend his day of leisure. It was here that he had discovered Marcus Aurelius. Papolic was obviously well disciplined, a conscientious and intellectually alert young man. I obtained further training manuals for his use, and I would be amazed if he did not make a chief's rating rather quickly.

Manelli was an immigrant's son from Philadelphia. He was slight of build but very solid; he gave the appearance of being a boxer, but had a sensitive side. Someone in the crew had acquired a record parodying Adolph Hitler called "Der Fuhrer's Face." He played this loud and raucous song in the crew's quarters incessantly. It finally proved too much for the musical Manelli. Grabbing the record from the player, he smashed it on the deck. He offered, however, to reimburse the sailor who had bought it, and told him that he just could not stand to hear it any longer. Behind the tough guy image was a very different and sensitive Manelli.

I remember the sailor who was the son of a West Virginia coal miner and whose previous life had been lived in a very grubby environment. He was introduced to cleanliness in the Navy, and he became her worshiper. He could break down and clean a gun and emerge from this dirty job himself spotless and unsoiled. I also re-member the former supermarket clerk who wrote his wife the most beautiful and tender love letters imaginable. I never hated more the job of having to censor my sailors' outgoing mail than when I found myself invading this man's letters to his wife.

Grilli, the baker on the *Young America*, loved his art. His pri-mary responsibility was to supervise the baking in the troop galley, most of the labor for which was provided by drafts of men from the troops aboard. He had an extraordinary capacity to produce fine baked goods in what would appear to be unlikely surroundings. He enjoyed nothing better than to bake a cake, a work of art, for me to bring to the port director's office on Oahu, where Grilli's reputa-tion was known.

I remember also Mays, the farm boy who had become a gun-ner's mate on the *Cristobal*. Early in America's participation in the war, Mays had belonged to a small detail of enlisted men without an officer assigned to man machine guns on a freighter. While in an English port he had been taken to a nearby Navy gunnery instal-lation and given target practice with machine guns under British tutelage. He had then been sent back to his ship, which sailed later that day. As the sun was setting, a plane was spotted coming toward his ship on the beam, flying low over the water, typical of the ap-proach one would expect from a German bomber. The plane gave no recognition signals and continued on its course.

Mays concluded that it was an enemy plane, and the ship was indeed in an area where this was quite possible. He opened fire with his machine gun. As the plane swerved so that its outline could be seen, he was horrified to recognize it as a British bomber just as it crashed into the sea. The plane had obviously not followed proper procedure in approaching the ship. Mays subsequently received from the British Navy a letter of recommendation for his marks-manship. Even so, the incident remained for him deeply disturb-ing, enough to bring tears to his eyes as he recalled the episode. I was always impressed by the sensitivity and understanding he had about men in the crew, coupled with a quiet maintenance of firm control over the situation assured by the respect in which he was held by the sailors.

My Navy experience heightened my realization of how important it is to understand the values that move and guide people in their lives. However valuable vocational or technical training may be, it is equally important to develop a sensitivity to the values that move men to action. My Navy experience thus heightened my sense of the importance of a liberal education. One can hardly regard active duty in war as a recommended way of education when one considers the injuries and deaths produced in such conflicts. Yet when, in 1946, I resumed my pilgrimage through universities, I did not think that my four-year stint in the Navy was irrelevant to the years I had spent in universities before 1942. Nor were those four Navy years to be irrelevant to the years I was to spend in universities after 1946.

Return to
Academe,
1946–1948

BY THE END OF THE FIRST WEEK IN JANUARY 1946,
Betty, our two-and-a-half-year-old daughter Mary Ann, and I were
driving in a heavily loaded car eastward across Arizona, New Mexico, and Texas and then north toward Urbana, Illinois. The house
we had built in Urbana in 1941 had been leased during the war years
to the Navy officer in command of a naval training unit, but it was
soon available for our very happy return to it.

By 1945 five of my articles on the Middle Ages had been published in *Speculum,* and what was essentially my doctoral thesis,
Vassi and Fideles in the Carolingian Empire, had been published as
volume 19 in Harvard Historical Monograph by the Harvard University Press. I decided in February 1946 to turn from the intro-
ductory course to European history I had taught before the war to
a course for upperclassmen and a graduate seminar on medieval
history.

As a means of increasing my own perspective on the Middle
Ages, I identified over a dozen members of the Illinois faculty in a
variety of departments who had an established interest in some as-

pect of medieval culture. I then sought opportunities for conversation with them as individuals to discuss the possibility of scheduling occasional dinner sessions to discuss a paper presented by a member of the group. Despite a wide range of responses from positive to very negative, I reserved a small dining room at the Men's University Club for a given evening and sent notices to my list of individuals. To my great delight every person I had spoken to came to the dinner and the medieval group was off to a good start, enriching perspectives on medieval times and culture for the participants. This group interaction about the Middle Ages was destined to continue for at least a couple of decades after I left the University of Illinois.

Returning veterans of World War II provided a substantial infusion of older students in 1946 and thereafter. Those who had served in Europe, having had an opportunity to see ancient and medieval monuments, were often curious about these earlier historical eras and their cultures. Some had actually studied a year or two of Latin, but needed to refurbish or expand their reading ability. I failed to arouse the interest of professors in the Classics Department in undertaking such a plan for students of history.

I encountered two students, Army veterans, who had developed an interest in the Middle Ages, and had earlier taken two years of Latin in high school. Remembering my own experience as a freshman at Dartmouth when Professor Nemiah invited a small group to his home for sight reading of a medieval Latin chronicle of the First Crusade, I resolved to attempt a similar effort with the participation of some fellow professors. A professor of political science had developed an interest in medieval political theory and wished to improve his skill in reading relevant Latin texts. A professor of English with a particular interest in the Celts in medieval Britain wished to join the group. A professor of German literature, along with one of his students, expressed interest in participating, and I had my two students of history who were eager to expand their ability to read medieval Latin texts. I proposed that we meet with regularity from eight to ten o'clock on Thursday evenings at my home during the regular academic year. Betty provided some light refreshments at the end of each session. These meetings continued until my departure from the University of Illinois in mid-1948.

My two student participants were exceptionally able. The younger one was an undergraduate, Eugene Brucker. During World War II the Rhodes Scholarship program had been suspended, but it was reestablished by the time Brucker completed his undergraduate degree, and he was named a Rhodes scholar. I remember advising him to use his two years at Oxford to broaden and deepen his knowledge of history, and to return to the United States for a Ph.D. degree from an American university. He did that, obtaining his doctorate from Princeton University with a focus on the Renaissance. For many years now he has been professor of Renaissance history at the University of California, Berkeley.

The slightly older student was Richard Sullivan, who completed his Ph.D. in medieval history at Illinois under me and then entered upon a distinguished career at Michigan State University as professor, chairman of the history department, dean of Arts and Sciences, and associate provost. He was one of the founders of what is now the International Congress of Medieval Studies, which meets every year during the spring break on the campus of Western Michigan University in Kalamazoo.

It is hard to comprehend the vast array of issues, problems, and readjustments the nation, and universities in particular, faced not only to effect the return to civilian life of the eleven million men who had been in active military service itself, but also to help millions of civilians return to a peacetime economy. At Illinois the administrative officers and the faculty bodies faced a host of problems. In 1946 and 1947, I found myself at the same time a member of the Executive Committee of the College of Arts and Sciences, of the Board of the Graduate School, and of the Educational Policy Committee of the Faculty Senate. The last committee was facing the challenge of establishing branch campuses to accommodate the surging applications for enrollment of returning veterans. While I was not moved by any self-conscious plan, in retrospect it is clear that I became involved in a succession of activities which gradually extended my contact with scholars beyond history to other disciplines in the humanities and social sciences.

I had begun teaching at the University of Illinois in September 1937 as an instructor in history for a ten-month salary of $2,000. I could supplement my income by teaching two months in the summer for a proportional salary. My ten-month salary was increased to $2,200 in September 1939. I was promoted to the rank of associate in September 1941 at $2,450 but was soon granted leave for service in the Navy in April 1942. In September 1945, while still on active duty in the Navy, I was promoted to associate professor on indefinite tenure at $3,800 for the ten-month academic year. I was able to return from the Navy to Illinois on January 21, 1946, for that salary, which was increased to $4,000 on September 1, 1946, and to $5,500 on September 1, 1947.

Six months later, on February 1, 1948, a major change in my status occurred because of a request from Dr. Ridenour, the newly appointed dean of the Graduate School. He was a brilliant physicist who had been much involved during World War II in scientific research for the Defense Department. Concerned that he might become too preoccupied with science and technology, Dean Ridenour wished to have in his office someone to watch out for the welfare particularly of the humanities. He suggested that I come half-time into his office as an assistant to him, and serve half-time as associate professor of history, effective February 1, 1948, at a total salary of $7,700. Some months later, on June 4, I was promoted to the rank of professor of history and assistant to the dean of the Graduate School at a salary of $9,000.

During my service at Illinois I found my colleagues in history to be very congenial partners, and the chairmen of the department in succession, Professors Robertson and Pease, to be friendly and considerate of my welfare. Through my committee assignments I came to know personally the president and higher academic administrators of the University of Illinois and to have respect for them. I could not have prophesized in early June 1948 that on August 9, 1948, I would write my friendly neighbor, President Grove Stoddard, the following letter:

I hereby submit my resignation from the University of Illinois so that I may accept the position of Executive Director, American Council of Learned Societies. I request that I be relieved of my duties as Professor of History and Assistant to the Dean of the Graduate College as of September 1, 1948. Dean Ridenour, Dean Larson, and Professor Pease have told me that they would interpose no objection to my release at that time.

It was not easy for me to come to this decision. My years as a member of the Department of History had been happy and rewarding. Professor Pease has given every opportunity to develop my own lines of interest and encouraged my sense of responsibility within the department. He has been quick to supply my needs and to advance my interests. I have always known that I had loyal support, and no one can value lightly that conviction. My more recent association with Dean Ridenour has been stimulating and interesting and personally gratifying. I have, therefore, come to my decision with a sense of great regret at leaving friends, with gratitude for the years past, and with a realization of my deep and abiding affection for and loyalty to the University of Illinois.

On May 8, 1948, Professor Joseph Strayer, the Princeton medievalist well known to me from Medieval Academy meetings, had written me that he was chairman of a search committee seeking candidates for the position of executive director of the American Council of Learned Societies (ACLS), and that his committee would like me to be among the finalists. A letter of June 23 asked me to meet in Washington, D.C., on June 26 for luncheon with the Board of Directors and in the afternoon with the selection committee. On July 23, I was notified that I was the unanimous choice of the Board as the next executive director of the ACLS. On August 9, I sent to President Stoddard my letter of resignation from the University of Illinois effective September 1, 1948.

The ACLS
Provides a
Multiuniversity
Exposure,
1948–1952

WHAT WAS THIS ORGANIZATION WHOSE FULL NAME WAS
the American Council of Learned Societies Devoted to Humanistic Studies? A bit of history may be helpful. Until the Civil War no
intellectual disciplines cultivated by American universities and colleges had achieved national sponsorship or financial support until
the federal government in 1863 chartered the National Academy of
Sciences to establish a means of consultation, primarily with natural scientists and technologists, about its weaponry and its conduct of the Civil War.

Subsequently, as the threat increased in 1916 of U.S. involvement in World War I, the federal government added the National
Research Council to the structure of the National Academy of Sciences. With only rare exceptions these agencies were focused on the
study of nature, aspects of the natural world around man, but not
on human beings as highly social creatures and also as distinct individuals. This national scientific structure was in place and again
provided great advances in American technology and weaponry
developed during the conduct of World War I.

When the four victorious heads of state gathered at Versailles to impose a treaty on the defeated powers, they faced a different set of problems from those posed by the technologies developed during the actual conduct of the war. The nineteenth century had been an imperial century for the major victorious European powers. They had established political control over many kinds of peoples, diverse in culture and language and distributed on other continents and islands in the oceans. Even the United States, as an aftermath of its earlier Spanish-American War, had acquired former Spanish possessions in Central America and in Southeast Asia. It was not to scientists but to students of human cultures, linguists, historians, political scientists, anthropologists, humanists, and social scientists, that the victorious heads of state had to turn for the knowledge base relevant to their decisions at Versailles as to the political reconfiguration of their empires.

The European powers had well-established multidisciplinary national academies to whose professorial members they could turn for information and advice relative to the imperial governance of diverse peoples on the globe. The United States, however, lacked such a national organization. Therefore, they had to send invitations to specific individual scholars, generally university professors from relevant human and social disciplines, who came to Versailles to be available to the American representatives for advice as they made decisions with the other heads of state as to who would rule whom and where.

While these academic advisers from the United States were so engaged, they also discussed with academic representatives of the victorious European powers the idea of creating an international academic body whose members could meet periodically for scholarly exchanges. This led quickly to establishment of the International Union of Academies, better known through its French version as the UAI, with an executive office in Brussels, Belgium.

When the American professors returned to the United States, some of them took the initiative to create an American Council of Learned Societies Devoted to Humanistic Studies—the ACLS, in short. Charles Homer Haskins, dean of the Harvard Graduate School and the medievalist under whom a decade later I would hope to be a student, was a prominent figure during the treaty making at Versailles and in the establishment of the ACLS in 1919. He served as chairman of the Board of Directors for its first five years. The chief staff officer, Waldo Leland, was executive director from 1919 until his retirement in 1946. He was succeeded in 1946–47 by Richard Shryock as acting director and in 1947–48 by Cornelius Kruse as executive director. The latter's decision in midyear to return to his professorship in philosophy at Wesleyan University created the opening as executive director, which I assumed on September 1, 1948.

The constituent societies at the time of my involvement with the ACLS numbered twenty-four, half of which could be considered representative of the humanities and half of the social sciences because of the latter's growing emphasis on quantitative studies. In 1929 the Social Science Research Council was created also to serve the social sciences, but many of the latter societies continued to retain also their connection with the ACLS. To deal with some problem areas, joint ACLS-SSRC committees have been established over the years.

The leaders of the ACLS had early turned their attention to what came to be called planning activities. They recognized topics that needed investigation but which often involved cross-disciplinary collaboration not only within one institution but with scholars in one or more other institutions. The international scope of World War I had initiated a growing interest among American scholars beyond their knowledge of Western European cultures to include what came to be called area studies devoted to languages and cultures of Eastern Europe, Africa, Asia, South America, and various islands. This interest was greatly expanded in World War II by the even greater involvement of Americans in that worldwide conflict.

At the time I became connected with the ACLS in 1948, the Council was deeply concerned with fostering area studies: Chinese and Japanese, Indic and Iranian, Slavic, Turkish, and Near Eastern. The growing sense of the Cold War with the Soviet Union and the need to know more about developments behind the Iron Curtain led early in my tenure to the publishing, under ACLS and SSRC auspices, of the 70,000 word weekly English translation of the *Current Digest of the Soviet Press*. Each edition included the full text of the two leading Soviet newspapers, *Pravda* and *Izvestia*, and selections from some forty other newspapers and journals. I remember that it was soon described by a leading American journalist as the biggest hole in the Iron Curtain. The ACLS also began publication of English translations of a series of books about contemporary Russia.

The ACLS also sponsored joint planning committees with cooperation from the appropriate national disciplinary organizations such as the Joint Committee on American Native Languages and the Committee for the Recovery of Archaeological Remains. It also brought together scholars from various universities concerned with Negro Studies, the History of Religions, Renaissance Studies, and American Civilization.

Before my arrival in 1948 the ACLS had acquired funds to award first-year fellowships to about thirty college graduates who showed interest and aptitude for a possible academic career in the humanities. In 1948 the ACLS, with a paid staff of seven persons and a tremendous amount of volunteer help from university and college faculty members, was still providing, on a relatively small financial basis, support for scholarship about human culture. Its funding came from such private philanthropic funds as the Rockefeller Foundation, the Carnegie Foundation, and the Bollingen Fund. At the same time, the natural sciences were receiving funding of a far different order of magnitude from the federal government in addition to grants from private sources.

Selective Service, the Student Draft, and the Humanities

I COULD NOT HAVE KNOWN in advance that I was to enter Washington, D.C., at a time of remarkable new developments in the establishment of organizations and programs broadly concerned with the pursuit of new knowledge. One such was the Conference Board of Associated Research Councils. Its members were the American Council on Education (for universities and colleges), the National Research Council (for the natural sciences), the Social Science Research Council, and the American Council of Learned Societies (for the humanities). I arrived in Washington in late August 1948 to participate in discussions with the leaders of this group.

One issue we faced was the impact of the military draft on college and university students. From 1940 to 1946 the induction of men into the military services, or their deferral or exemption, was controlled by the Selective Service Act of 1940. Under that Act, decisions on deferral or exemption were made on an individual basis, the responsibility largely in the hands of the local draft boards. Aside from deferments or exemptions for hardship or other personal reasons, they could be granted because of the individual's "essentiality" for the war effort. When students were granted deferments by the local boards on the basis of their involvement in fields deemed essential, it was generally because they were studying the natural sciences, engineering, or medicine. By January 1947, however, the War Department had enough volunteers to cease calls for men to Selective Service, and on March 31 the Act itself expired.

The aggressiveness of the Soviet Union and Fifth Columnist activity soon heightened the sense of an evolving Cold War, and in March 1948 President Truman requested the enactment of the Selective Service Act of 1948, which became law June 24. It authorized the president by regulation to provide for deferment from service of any college or university student for such time as he deemed appropriate. The previous director of Selective Service, General Lewis Hershey, found himself director again of a program to provide selection of men "which is fair and just, and which is consistent with the maintenance of an effective national economy." The law also declared that national security required "maximum effort in the fields of scientific research and development, and the fullest possible utilization of the nation's technological, scientific, and other critical manpower resources."

Six committees were named by General Hershey on August 20, 1948, representing in their membership experience in the fields of engineering, the biological and physical sciences, the healing arts, the social sciences, and the humanities. I had barely arrived in Washington when I found myself a member and chairman of the humanities committee. On a morning in early November, five committees met in the Selective Service offices for briefing by members of General Hershey's staff. The healing arts committee had already met separately and submitted its recommendations to Hershey.

At the noon break, the social scientists and biologists met for lunch separately, but the three other committees—the physical scientists, the engineering scientists, and the humanists—joined for lunch together in a private dining room at the nearby Cosmos Club. A very interesting discussion emerged about the types of deferment that would probably have been granted by the specialist groups during World War II. Speculation led to the conclusion that the theoretical physicists of the type who led the way to the atom bomb would probably not have been considered a year or two before the actual beginning of World War II as sufficiently involved in war work to warrant their deferral. The humanists pointed out the probability of a similar negative reaction to the utility of Japanese scholars in the early phases of World War II.

When the five groups returned in the afternoon to the Selective Services office, they joined in one meeting and requested that the healing arts committee join them in the future. It was also proposed that someone be appointed to chair the joint meetings of the committees. M. H. Trytten, director of the Office of Scientific Personnel of the National Research Council, was appointed chairman. He had ample experience during World War II with the problems of student deferments, and he was a good chairman for the whole group. By December 21, 1948, the six committees in their joint meetings had come to a joint recommendation which was submitted to General Hershey and passed by him to the Executive Branch. At that very moment the sense of emergency evaporated. The January 1949 draft call was cut in half to 5,000, and the February 1949 call was canceled and inductions came to a halt.

On June 25, 1950, however, North Korea without warning attacked South Korea. On June 30, President Truman extended the Selective Service Act to July 9, 1951, and the issue of student deferment was returned to the agenda as the nation again faced an expansion in its security effort. Americans were already fighting in Korea when in October and November 1950 the six Selective Service committees met again, as a committee of the whole, to review and reaffirm its earlier recommendations. I was called upon to serve as chairman of the drafting committee. Dr. Trytten, as our chairman, and I presented the results to General Hershey. These recommendations were far from what he had expected when he appointed the six committees in 1948, but he accepted the reasons behind them and became supportive of them.

Arrangements were made to present the recommendations to a large audience on December 18, 1950, and I was asked to explain the line of thought behind them. The essence appears in the following quotation from my presentation to the audience:

Proponents of the plan preserving a flow of personnel for the "essential" sciences are quick to state the essentiality of the fields of learning with which they are themselves concerned, though as reasonable men they generally recognize that there are other fields which also may be essential. Even so, such proposals are to be viewed as somewhat irresponsible until their proponents are willing to state and document that "these are the essential fields of learning," and "those are the nonessential fields." If any group elects to present such a list and it becomes the basis of national policy, it must be remembered that the very list will form and shape things to come, largely extinguishing some fields of knowledge or stopping their growth, and predetermining the lines of the nation's scientific and cultural development in the coming years. It will also predetermine the sciences and skills available to us for our defense. The nation which had guessed wrong could easily be all wrong if this policy is followed.

What the committees did recommend was that differences in human abilities should be recognized and that the needs of the military establishment and of the supporting activities of the nation require a flow of competently trained specialists who could only come from the universities and colleges. If the members must be limited, then we should choose those to continue in college not on the basis of risky judgments as to the essentiality of fields of study, but on the probability of their individual capacity to complete the study of their specializations, on their educational aptitude defined as a specified minimum score on a general classification test, and on a record of previous educational accomplishment sufficiently high to indicate promise of eventual scientific or specialized competence.

The 82nd Congress opened in early January 1951, and I remember feeling that the Selective Service committee report had attracted little attention and that the big guns were still speaking of national security as though it were subsumed under military defense and exclusively a matter of military hardware. Somewhere I heard that there was an intelligent young political scientist on President Truman's staff, small then in comparison with later times. He was Harold Enarson, later to be staff head of the Western Interstate Commission for Higher Education (WICHE) and subsequently president of Cleveland State University and then of Ohio State University. In early January 1951, I invited Enarson to luncheon at the old Willard Hotel, and described to him the recommendations of the Selective Service committees and the reasons therefore.

Late on January 18, 1951, I received a mimeographed copy of the proposed USMT legislation and to my surprise learned that the

70,000 persons annually who could be selected to engage in study or research could do so "in medicine, the sciences, engineering, the humanities, and other fields determined by him (the President) to be in the national interest." I subsequently learned from Enarson that he had been persuaded of the wisdom of the recommendations of the Selective Service Committees and had so presented them to President Truman's legal counsel, who in turn presented the arguments to President Truman. The president, in turn convinced, had instructed the Department of Defense to write the word "humanities" into the original list of "medicine, science, engineering, and other fields."

That same evening I was scheduled to attend a dinner hosted by Arthur Adams, president of the American Council on Education. Adams was nervous about the difference of opinion over the draft among educators, and particularly about the probable conflict of opinion between me and James Bryant Conant, then president of Harvard University, who was also scheduled to speak the following morning at the opening session of the delegates from the university and college members of the ACE. It transpired that evening that earlier that day Conant had received from Senator Leverett Saltonstall the same mimeographed copy of the USMT bill and had decided to accept it, thus backing down from his earlier position. Hence, no real confrontation between him and me took place the next day. The insertion of "humanities" into the scientific and technical list was to prove ultimately a death blow to the essential fields approach to the matter of student deferments. It eliminated the need to decide which fields were sufficiently essential to warrant the granting of deferments.

It was still far from clear what Congress would do. I was finally scheduled to appear before the Senate Preparedness Subcommittee on January 30, 1951. As I awaited my turn to testify, the committee continued to fall behind its schedule. The chairman, Senator Lyndon Johnson, was obviously concerned about the hour when he called me. He asked me if I had a prepared statement. I replied that I did. Since I had in mind a procedure to capture the attention of the committee members which I felt would be lost if I could not make an oral report to them, I indicated my unhappiness.

Senator Johnson yielded, saying, "Will you please proceed." I responded, "I appreciate the opportunity, sir," and then proceeded with my testimony in which I focused on the text of the draft bill, calling attention to the inclusion as grounds for student deferments of the word "humanities" along with medicine, science, and engineering. I expressed support for the inclusion in the bill of such deferments of students, and argued in particular the case for including opportunities for continued studies by students of man and his works.

On leaving my office that morning I had picked up some objects to illustrate my point. I placed on the table manuals for learning spoken Russian, Korean, Japanese, and Serbo-Croatian while justifying the continued need for training persons for describing and teaching foreign languages. I presented the *Political Dictionary in Russian*, a handbook for political organizers developed by Russians for their own use, suggesting that the senators would find interesting the English translation of the definition of "democracy" in this Russian book. I presented an *Economic Geography of the USSR* written by Russians for their own uses, and a survey of *Soviet Views on the Post-War World Economy*. I noted that a passage in Vishinsky's *The Law of the Soviet State* in an English translation had been used by the U.S. delegate to the United Nations, Mrs. Franklin Delano Roosevelt, to controvert a statement by the then Russian Foreign Minister Vishinsky, who was the author of the book. I placed before the senators some copies of *The Current Digest of the Soviet Press*, described by a prominent commentator as "the biggest hole there is in the Iron Curtain."

I asserted finally that the operations of the experts capable of producing such materials were directly related to the intelligent handling of immediate and vital problems of defense. Therefore I approved the inclusion of the humanities in the areas of research designated in the bill and urged the adoption of a policy that would permit the nation to have at least a minimum number of persons trained in many fields.

With my closing words the chairman banged his gavel on the table and left the room. The other members, however, all remained for some time, commenting and asking questions about the material I had brought to the meeting. They were positive in their attitude, two of them remarking that my testimony was the first to touch upon the humanities. Senator John Stennis a few days later wrote me, "I was much impressed by your fine testimony before the Senate Preparedness Subcommittee." Senator Harry Cain wrote, "I was interested in your statement before the Committee because it broadened my knowledge, and I am hopeful that the Committee will include the phrase, *the humanities,* and make reference to it in the Committee Report. I have sent my own word of encouragement to the Committee and perhaps this will help." The chairman, Senator Johnson, wrote, "Your testimony before the Preparedness Subcommittee was of real significance and will be very helpful to us. We deeply appreciate the cooperation."

The bill emerged from the Armed Services Committee with the wording intact to permit deferments for students "to engage in study or research in medicine, dentistry, osteopathy, the sciences, engineering, the humanities and other fields determined by (the President) to be in the national interest." This language remained in the bill as it passed the Senate. By the time the House of Representatives had taken up the matter of the draft, General Hershey had more prominently identified his own plan for student deferments. He followed the recommendations of his committees in avoiding the essential fields approach. He proposed employing class standing and tests scores as a means of determining eligibility for deferment, not in combination as recommended by the committees, but on an either-or basis. A conference committee between the House and Senate finally led to the final Act of Congress in 1951 that followed the House version, which implicitly recognized the humanities and social sciences as serving important national interests, permitting deferments for the study of them as well as the sciences and engineering.

Six years later, the launching by the Soviet Union of its first Earth satellite on October 4, 1957, stirred up again a great reaction in this country, arousing fear for the adequacy of our defense and of our capacity to compete with the Russians in sciences, technology, and this time modern foreign languages. To provide the necessary assistance, the Congress passed in September 1958 the National Defense Education Act whose preamble states:

We must increase our efforts to identify and educate more of the talent of our Nation. This requires programs that will give assurance that no student of ability will be denied an opportunity for a higher education because of financial need; and that will correct as rapidly as possible the existing imbalances in our educational program which have led to insufficient proportions of our population educated in science, mathematics, and modern foreign languages, and trained in technology.

Foreign area study programs were particularly cited for support. The humanities, in part at least, had entered an era of federal financial aid because of their relation to what was perceived as defense needs.

The door of federal aid was opened still further for the humanities and arts too on more general grounds of national welfare with the passage in 1965 of the act authorizing the National Endowment for the Humanities and the National Endowment for the Arts. At the initial meeting on this legislation the first speaker was the Secretary of Health, Education and Welfare. As the then chairman of the American Council on Education, I was the second or third witness to testify, of course on behalf of the bill.

Following passage of the bill by Congress it was sent to President Lyndon Johnson for his action. I was invited to the White House to witness the president's signing. A number of pens were on the desk beside him. He used them *seriatim* as he signed his name. At one point he reached for a pen to write the second "n" in Lyndon. He then handed me that pen. We had both seen at least some improvements in the valuation of the humanities in the United States. I delivered that pen for the second "n" in "Lyndon" to the University of Washington Library for safekeeping.

A Concern for America's Resources in Human Talent

THE ISSUES INVOLVED in granting deferments from the draft to college and university students during World War II had focused attention on the nation's need for highly qualified graduates in many specialized fields of knowledge. The National Research Council arm of the National Academy of Sciences had acquired some experience in making relevant studies of the status of the sciences and technologies, but there had been little comparable work for the humanities and social sciences.

It had became obvious to me by 1949 at the ACLS that there was a need for the Council to examine the future needs for humanists and social scientists not only for colleges and universities, but for government. No one on the Council staff had the appropriate training, but I found in the U.S. Employment Service a manpower specialist with the requisite background, J. F. Wellemeyer. With help from foundation funds I was able to bring him to the ACLS offices in September 1949, where he produced a number of useful manpower studies with reference to humanists and social scientists.

The advent of the Cold War had previously led the four national research councils (American Council of Learned Societies, American Council on Education, National Research Council, and Social Science Research Council) jointly to see the wisdom of undertaking a systematic study of the full array of diverse but talented persons emerging from colleges and universities. Accordingly their Conference Board of Associated Research Councils obtained from the Rockefeller Foundation a preliminary grant of $20,000 for a feasibility study in May 1947.

133

I arrived as executive director of the ACLS in late August 1948
in time to participate in the decision to continue with the study
and to request ultimately $240,000 as an additional grant from the
Rockefeller Foundation. The grant and supervision of the study
were placed by the Conference Board under a Commission on Human Resources and Advanced Training, of which I was appointed
chairman, and Merriam H. Trytten, my excellent colleague, was appointed vice chairman.

It was our extreme good fortune to persuade Dael Wolfle, then
the executive secretary of the American Psychological Association,
to undertake in 1950 the role of director of the study, which cul-
minated in 1954 in the landmark volume *America's Resources of
Specialized Talent: A Current Appraisal and a Look Ahead.* Subsequently Dr. Wolfle served from 1954 to 1970 as the executive director of the American Association for the Advancement of Science. I
am happy to note that he was then persuaded in 1970 to come to
the University of Washington to serve as a professor of public affairs until his retirement in 1977.

An Intensive Introduction
to Academic Affairs Abroad

YET ANOTHER ASPECT of my four years' experience at the ACLS
was my exposure to university affairs in a number of countries
in Europe, Asia, and Latin America. I arrived at the Washington
offices of the ACLS toward the end of August 1948 at the time of
burgeoning international activity concerning universities and intellectual interchange. The United Nations Educational, Scientific,
and Cultural Organization (UNESCO) had become an adjunct of
the United Nations in 1946. There had long been an active International Council of Scientific Unions, but there was no such international body for the humanities and social sciences. UNESCO
therefore initiated the creation of the International Council of Philosophy and Humanistic Studies (ICPHS) to encourage research

and to plan international conferences dealing with the disciplines concerned with people and their cultures.

The ICPHS held its first meeting in Brussels on January 18– 21, 1949. One of the constituent members of the ICPHS was the International Union of Academies, represented at that first Brussels meeting by delegates from academies of Western European countries and by a delegate from the United States, William Berrien of the ACLS. I myself served as a delegate of the ACLS to the International Union of Academies in June 1949 and again in 1950. From 1949 to 1955 I was a member of the Board of the U.S. National Commission of UNESCO. From 1952 to 1959 I was vice-president of the International Council for Philosophy and Humanistic Studies, and from 1959 to 1965 its president. These assignments provided me with a rich opportunity to meet with professors from universities in many countries and to chair sessions of the ICPHS in succession in Ann Arbor, Tokyo, Mexico City, and Amsterdam.

Dean of Arts
and Sciences at the
University of Michigan,
1952–1958

EARLY IN 1948, MY FIRST YEAR AT THE ACLS, I HAD begun visits to the larger research-oriented universities, the first of which was the University of Michigan, where Dean Keniston of the College of Literature, Science, and the Arts had been a very helpful host in introducing me to a fine institution. I was pleased to be invited later to the university's Annual Conference on Higher Education on November 27, 1951, to speak on "The Function of a College." Dean Keniston was about to retire, and in early March 1952, I was asked to come again to Ann Arbor to meet with the search committee and the university officers to discuss the deanship. By May 6, 1952, my appointment as Dean and Professor of History at Michigan had been confirmed by the regents.

Several weeks later, Betty and I traveled to Ann Arbor to investigate housing. After a discouraging day we went to the Kenistons' pleasant New England style house for tea and conversation with our hosts. The women soon wandered off, leaving their husbands involved in academic talk. They finally returned to us, to report that they had toured the house and agreed upon its suitability for the Odegaards' needs. The outcome was that the Kenistons were prepared to suggest a reasonable price for its sale to us. Betty and I were delighted to accept the offer of what proved to be a comfortable residence in a pleasant neighborhood near an elementary school for our daughter to attend.

The Odegaard family had barely settled in the former Keniston house when I was called upon in late September 1952 to speak at the dedication of two new classroom buildings that replaced ancient buildings but retained the names of the predecessors. One had been named for Stevens T. Mason, the first governor of Michigan, who had persuaded the State Legislature to appropriate funds in 1841 enabling the regents to bring into existence the College of Literature, Science, and the Arts, the oldest of the units of the University of Michigan, and indeed the main trunk from which other units had sprung. Two of the Literary College's faculty, the professor of zoology and botany and the professor of chemistry, mineralogy, and geology, had been the ones who took the initiative in proposing plans for the Medical School; and they were its first professors when instruction in medicine began in 1850. This was the first of a notable series of cases in which the L.S.&A. faculty recognized needs and undertook to meet them by providing appropriate instruction within its shelter until the time might come to establish independent units. In addition to L.S.&A., Medicine and Law had been contemplated by the Legislature in 1837 as possible schools, and they had long come into existence by my time at Michigan in the 1950s.

There had also emerged from L.S.&A. by that time professional schools in Engineering, Pharmacy, Education, Natural Resources, Business Administration, and Social Work. Meanwhile the Literary College faculty had developed graduate instruction for the M.A. and Ph.D. degrees offered by many of its departments in the physical and biological sciences, the social sciences, and the humanities. This listing simply illustrates how the Literary faculty had been involved in a growing web of interaction with other faculties of the university.

The Governance of the Literary College

A NEWCOMER AS DEAN to the literary college in 1952 could not fail to be impressed by the specificity of the stated provisions for governance of academic business contained in its seventy-page Faculty Code. In the 1940s a review of past actions in faculty meetings and of administrative practices in the College had led by 1947 to the drafting of the first Code. A second revision was well under way when I arrived in 1952 and was published in April 1954. The Code provided for regular meetings of the Governing Faculty on the first Monday in each month throughout the ten-month academic year, except in January and June.

The membership of the Governing Faculty comprised professors, associate professors, assistant professors, instructors, and resident lecturers with professorial rank in the College. The dean was the designated chairman of the Governing Faculty, which was described as "in charge of the affairs of the College except to the extent that such affairs are hereinafter placed in charge of the Dean and Executive Committee." The latter important body was described as follows:

The executive functions of the College shall be performed by the Dean assisted by an Executive Committee. The Executive Committee is charged with the duty of investigating and formulating educational and instructional policies for consideration by the Faculty and it shall act for the College in matters related to the budgets, promotions, and appointments.

The Executive Committee shall consist of the Dean and six members to be appointed by the Board of Regents on recommendation by the President. The Dean shall be chairman of the Committee. The Associate Dean and the dean in charge of student matters in this College shall sit with the Committee but shall be without vote. The Associate Dean shall act as secretary to the Committee.

At the spring meeting of the Faculty, the members nominated faculty to be considered for the Executive Committee and then cast their votes in a secret ballot. For each vacancy, the names of at least the three persons with the highest votes were then presented by the dean to the president, who could choose one of the three for the vacant position. In a memorandum written in July 1955, I wrote as follows:

The Executive Committee of the College is a working committee approaching over the year, I am sure, well over three hours of deliberation a week. In January and February, when promotions and merit increases are being considered, we may well meet three times a week for extended discussions. There is, first, the necessity of complete candor among the members of the Committee. Each member must be prepared to stand up and be counted even on the most difficult of issues. The second general principle is the rule of confidence by which the discussions within the committee are regarded as private. The results of actions, of course, inevitably become known in time. This leads to the third rule, namely, responsible support of the Committee's actions, much of which must be expressed by restraint and absence of comment even in the face of considerable inducement to speak freely.

There was one incident that illustrates the serious hold of these principles on members of the Executive Committee. They confronted a difficult issue and debated openly the pros and cons, but finally arrived at a statement that seemed to be accepted by all members. At the ensuing faculty meeting the statement was presented as the recommendation of the Executive Committee. To the surprise of all other members of the Committee, one member rose in opposition. After the ensuing discussion, a somewhat modified version was accepted by the Faculty. At the next meeting of the Executive Committee the other members simply did not speak to the offending member. The next day he came to my office, and broke down in tears. I told him that since he had not revealed his negative stance on the issue to his colleagues in our committee meeting, he would have to take the initiative in seeking peace with them.

Separate committees dealt with such matters as the curriculum, scholarships, admissions, and examinations, policy recommendations concerning which would be referred to the Governing Faculty via the dean and Executive Committee. It should be noted that the dean also served as chairman of the meetings of the Governing Faculty of the Literary College. The Faculty Code also provided:

The Faculty shall submit its communications to the Board of Regents in writing through the Dean and the President of the University. The Dean may, if he desires, supplement any such communication with any statements or explanations deemed by him desirable.

The office of the Dean shall be so organized that the Dean may be free to devote a large proportion of his time and energy to the continuous development of the educational and instructional policies of the College.

I believe that it must be said that I arrived at the University of Michigan at a time which permitted me to fall heir as dean to a responsive internal administrative structure that encouraged an unusual participation by faculty members in the development of policies. First, faculty committees at the lower level considered such matters as student admissions, curriculum, examinations, and student discipline. Their conclusions could then be referred to the dean and Executive Committee for possible subsequent presentation to the Governing Faculty of the College and then possible referral in some form to the President and Board of Regents for action.

After five years of observation of a system of unusual faculty participation in administrative processes, in my fifth annual report to the Literary Faculty on October 7, 1957, I commented as follows:

One sees many evidences in academic man now of the strain in him between two conflicting forces. On the one hand he is pushed in the direction of isolating individualism by the incessant curiosity and the independent, prying mind which fits him for the university as a place dedicated to the advancement of knowledge. To a considerable extent, in the pursuit of knowledge and in the communication of it to his students, he is to be the independent master of his situation. But at the same time it has been known for at least seven hundred years in those places where knowledge has usually been most assiduously cultivated that the scholar is less effective when he works alone than when he joins in a group of similarly dedicated souls, when he becomes part of a social institution created to advance and disseminate learning, when he becomes a member of a university. The invention of the university represents indeed the socialization of the learned profession. The very name used emphasizes the concept that the sum of the individuals has somehow become more than the sum of the parts. They have been turned into one, have become a corporation. The corporation can bring to the work of the individuals support and assistance of many kinds which the individuals on their own could not find. How obvious this is now as we look around us to see libraries, laboratories, and classrooms and the security of personal status which the university brings to its participating faculty.

A university requires of its members, then, apart from individual initiative and drive, social skills if it is to function effectively internally and in relation to the surrounding society. The academic person needs, in addition to competence in teaching and research, at least a modicum of what might be called corporate skills, or what is more commonly referred to as "administrative experience." In recent decades academics have been restive and uneasy about this matter. As universities have grown in size and complexity, the demands for such skills have increased. They will be required still more in the future. If the only consequence of increased size were increased need for administrative talent, we could perhaps count the process a dead loss. There are, fortunately, benefits resulting from size, among them greater social and financial support. One has only to contrast, in "opportunities for research," the complex university with the small college to see that there are some advantages in the larger institution. I believe that our profession would be well advised, if it wishes to encourage healthy universities, (1) to accept the legitimacy of administration as a requirement of the university as a social institution and (2) to accept experience and competence in administrative matters as a desirable component in every *homo academicus*. There has been a tendency in the academic world in general to leave too many corporate burdens to be analyzed and dealt with by too few members.

It is my observation, based on some effort to find out how other universities operate, that the University of Michigan and the

Literary College in particular were fortunate in the degree to which there existed a real participation by many in the concerns that affect all. Such a feeling in the last analysis cannot be given by any authority. There was in the University of Michigan a high degree of autonomy over many aspects of the program carried by lower echelons in the structure. Such delegation in a social institution can work smoothly only when it is matched by a high degree of responsibility over common concerns exercised at these lower levels. During my service there I sought to preserve the Literary College tradition of responsible faculty participation in administrative questions and to keep it alive through constant use.

It should be noted that the deans of the several schools and colleges of the University of Michigan met on approximately a monthly basis as the Deans Conference with the president and his senior officers for an exchange of information about matters of general interest. However, in the mid-1950s there was little in the way of administrative structure to provide for and encourage active discussion of faculty collaboration or partnerships among the schools and colleges.

By midcentury the heavy pressure particularly in research-oriented universities like Michigan toward specialization, and within an increasing number of academic departments, tended rather to encourage separation and lack of contact among specialists in the separated school faculties even when new perspectives and new relationships were possible and desirable. When I was invited to the University of Missouri during its Arts and Science Week in December 1952, I presented a speech on "The Unity of the Arts and Sciences," to urge the offering of a more liberal education in the undergraduate years.

Almost a year later, in October 1953, I followed this with a speech in Ann Arbor entitled "The Third Dimension." By the first dimension I meant the natural world, the physical environment within which, while life lasts, we move and have our being. But man is also a social animal; important to him beyond all other kinds in the world is the cultural bond with his own kind. The third dimension of human experience is the intimate and personal one, in which we are conscious of ourselves as individuals, seeking our own personal values and morals, our own identity even as we look out on the universe of other human beings and of nature.

However important specialized knowledge may be, I also wished to present the need for the many departments within Arts and Sciences to provide undergraduate students not only with an introduction to specialized knowledge, but with a liberal educational experience about the natural world, their fellow human beings, and their own identity. The faculty of the Literary College in many departments had already established a notable reputation for the research underpinning of its graduate degree programs and their quality.

As a means of ensuring more attention to the quality of the teaching available to undergraduate students, I urged the College faculty to develop a more general and liberal program for all undergraduate students which would include selected students for a special four-year Honors Program. I was fortunately able to persuade a highly respected member of the faculty, the distinguished sociologist Robert Angell, to accept the directorship. He had been president of both the national and the international associations of sociologists, but he also had a history of interest in undergraduate education, confirmed by his request that he be permitted to keep the directorship of the Honors Program for four years so that he could see the final record set by this first group of students.

Literary College Interaction with Other Schools and Colleges

AT THE TIME of my arrival as dean of the Literary College there was no higher administrative structure to participate in, or to facilitate discussion or planning among, the several schools and colleges of the university. The periodic Deans Conference Committee provided opportunities to hear reports about issues or events of general interest by President Harlan Hatcher, about the budget by Vice-President and Dean of Faculties Marvin Niehuss, and about buildings and plant or fiscal management problems by Vice-President for Business Wilbur Pierpont. These meetings did not include in my years at Michigan the opportunity to present and discuss particular problems or prospects that involved relations between the various academic units. It was left to me to negotiate relationships directly with other deans and faculty members.

Given the growing emphasis on specialization and the breadth of subject matters in the humanities, the social sciences, and the natural sciences pursued by the members of the Literary College faculty, it was inevitable that questions would arise about possible relationships between separate academic units on the campus. For example, the university had developed the following cluster of independent museums physically housed in the Museums Building: the Museum of Anthropology, the Kelsey Museum of Archaeology, the University Herbarium, the Museum of Paleontology, and the Museum of Zoology. Each dealt with subjects closely related to those of Literary College departments. To encourage closer relations with the College, in March 1956 the regents made the directors of all museums responsible to the dean and Executive Committee of the College. Once this administrative change had been effected, I made the director of each museum a member of the Executive Committee of the related department in the College as a means of effecting increased dialogue between museum and related department staffs.

Another separate entity was the Institute for Human Biology, whose director had developed a competent but disparate and isolated group of researchers. The director was at the point of retirement, and it fell to me to be appointed chairman of a committee to recommend the fate of the Institute. It seemed best to disband it as such even though its individual members were well qualified. It soon became evident that they could be advantageously placed individually elsewhere in the university. One of its members was asked to become chairman of a newly established Department of Genetics in the Medical School. Another of its younger members, an anthropologist, soon emerged as chairman of the Department of Anthropology. The others were placed in suitable faculty niches elsewhere in the university.

Another isolated organization appeared on the campus near the time of my own arrival in 1952, the Institute for Social Research. It was in origin a private corporation dependent for its economic survival on private or corporate grants or fees in support of opinion polling surveys produced by its corps of competent social scientists. They were primarily sociologists, psychologists, political scientists, and economists concerned with making as accurate as possible surveys on many kinds of issues. Professor Donald Marquis, chairman of the Department of Psychology, had urged recruitment of the Institute, still a private corporation, to a site on the Michigan campus in the hope of eventually establishing faculty status for some of its members in appropriate academic departments of the College. That process was under way during my deanship, enriching the research and teaching in the several social science departments through carefully determined faculty appointments of excellent recruits from the Institute. Some like Angus Campbell brought to the members of the College Curriculum Committee new insights about student reactions to College courses produced through student surveys conducted by him. The Institute and the members of its staff who became faculty members had a long and constructive history at the University of Michigan.

I remember a chance conversation one day with the chairmen of the physics and chemistry departments, who were both very critical of the poor introduction to science the freshmen students brought with them on entering the university. I asked them if they had ever made any inquiries directly or discussed this subject with school personnel or, indeed, with the dean of the College of Education. They confessed they had not, but they readily agreed to a meeting with the dean. In that subsequent conversation the two chairmen agreed to collaborate with the dean and some professors of education in developing for the next Summer Session a special course on teaching science at the high school level. An important by-product of this experience was the ensuing search by both chairmen to recruit for their departments a faculty member with an established interest in the teaching of science at the high school as well as college level.

A similar link was forged between the Literary College and the Medical School as a consequence of an initiative by the chairman of Zoology. He had recruited a couple of younger molecular biologists for his department. It became evident to me that they and some other biologists in the Literary College faculty might share interests with faculty members in the basic sciences of medicine. I sought a conversation with the dean of Medicine about this possibility and we jointly initiated a university committee on biology as a means of encouraging mutual interchanges among previously separated departments.

The Library and Other Space Problems

BY THE TIME of my arrival at the University of Michigan in 1952 the original acreage in the center of Ann Arbor set aside as the campus had been virtually filled with university buildings, while the surrounding area had been fully covered with privately owned business structures, apartments, houses, and some university dormitories. It had been decided that the original campus area should ultimately be used for the central administration and mostly for the College of Literature, Science, and the Arts. The occupants of the Medical School Building would be moved to new quarters some blocks away and close to the University Hospitals overlooking the Huron River.

Engineering, Music, and other smaller schools as well as more student housing would be established in a new area across the river on the new North Campus site. Meanwhile the Library was suffering from inadequate space even for storage, much less the use of books by faculty and students. My exposure to libraries as a student at Dartmouth and Harvard and as a faculty member at the University of Illinois hardly prepared me for the increasingly unmanageable library situation at Michigan. While at the ACLS in Washington D.C., I had the good fortune to have frequent exposure to the user-friendly Library of Congress and to its top executives, Luther Evans, the Librarian of Congress, and his associates Vernor Clapp and Frederick Wagman.

At Michigan the library lacked space for classifying and processing, let alone the mere storage of books that had been ordered and delivered. Faculty and students, if they obtained a desired book in the library and wished to read it there, often could not find an empty chair or carrel. Warner Rice, the University Librarian, could describe the chaos but not the cure. Meanwhile he also served as chairman of the very large English Department of the Literary College, which inevitably presented its own problems for his attention.

I had learned quickly at Michigan that when I was troubled by a problem needing some attention by higher authority I could easily gain access, depending on the subject matter, to Vice-Presidents Niehuss and Pierpont and to President Hatcher. In the case of the Library, I requested an appointment with the president through his secretary. She responded by arranging a meeting with him in the library of the President's House at the center of the Michigan campus. After a careful discussion of the situation, the president asked me to arrange a five-year term for Dr. Rice as chairman of the English Department, and he asked me to serve as chairman of a search committee to recommend a new librarian for the university.

That search ended in the fall of 1953 with the appointment of Frederick Wagman, one of the top officers of the Library of Congress. He had to develop a radically new plan for the Library's future, which he reported to the Literary Faculty in the fall of 1954. An earlier proposal to wrap a new structure around the Main Library had proved impracticable. A storage library for less frequently used books, which could be built on the North Campus, had become an obvious necessity. Libraries for schools like Engineering and Music which were to be transferred to the North Campus should be included within their new structures on the North Campus. The Medical School activities and its library housed in the Medical School Building on the Central Campus should be moved to new facilities near the hospital site, while the old Medical School Building itself would be used by the Literary College. A new library building housing a collection of books specifically chosen for undergraduate student education, providing adequate chairs and desks for students' use while reading, and serviced by an adequate reference staff should be planned.

A year later, in the fall of 1955, Professor Wagman reported that action on these several fronts was under way and that by the fall of 1956 the new Undergraduate Library would be open to serve students. He recognized that this new library institution could be a challenge to undergraduate faculty as well as to their students. He urged the faculty to go beyond reliance on textbooks to consider in particular new ways to guide students to use the richer resources that would be available in this new library. It was a great source of pleasure to me to see the enrichment of experience not only for students, but also for faculty, instigated by the opening of the Undergraduate Library at Michigan.

A Michigan Farewell

BETTY AND I had found ourselves very happy with our life in Ann Arbor as an attractive environment with pleasant neighbors and friends. We enjoyed very much our association with the University of Michigan, its officers, and its faculty. Our daughter Mary Ann was happy with her school and her friends. We had developed no enthusiasm or aspirations for life elsewhere. I had been approached about a possible interest in presidencies of liberal arts colleges and universities. I do remember one telephone call about midnight in snow-covered Ann Arbor when I was asked about my possible interest in the University of Hawaii; I hesitated maybe a second while I thought about the weather before I answered in the negative. I could not have prophesied that on January 29, 1958, I would accept appointment to the presidency of the University of Washington, effective August 29, 1958. But, as I will relate shortly, I did.

On May 5, 1958, I presided for the last time at the meeting of the Literary College faculty. At the end of the session, Professor H. R. Crane offered the following resolution:

WHEREAS the University has regretfully accepted the resignation of Dr. Charles E. Odegaard as Dean of the College of Literature, Science, and the Arts, to permit him to accept the presidency of the University of Washington, and

WHEREAS during his six years in his office he has rendered distinguished service to the College, the University, and the cause of education in the State of Michigan, and

WHEREAS by virtue of his educational statesmanship he has made many contributions to the College which have enhanced its scholarly prestige and educational programs,

THEREFORE BE IT RESOLVED that the Faculty of this College tender Dr. Odegaard a vote of thanks and appreciation for his labors in its behalf and offer him its best wishes for success in the years to come.

I expressed to the faculty my joy in working with them in what for me was a liberal education, and declared that their spirit would follow me in whatever endeavors I might pursue in the future.

From the
University of
Michigan to the
University of
Washington, 1958

ON THE MORNING OF OCTOBER 15, 1957, I RECEIVED A
telephone call at my Ann Arbor office from a Mr. Harold Shefelman, who identified himself as a regent of the University of Washington and chairman of its search committee charged with making
recommendations to the Board of Regents as to candidates for
president of that university. He expressed the hope that he could
see me in my office that afternoon. I told him that I harbored no
thoughts about leaving Michigan, and therefore doubted the utility to him of such a meeting.

In a very courteous manner he assured me that he would still
like to meet me. I did not, and could not, refuse to see him. I found
that I was to meet one of the most remarkable men of my lifetime,
one who could not fail to arouse a favoring response to his presentation of a case for the University of Washington. Born in Texas, as
an orphan he had worked his way through school to earn an undergraduate degree from Brown University and then a law degree from
Yale. Later he would be a trustee of Brown and a member of an advisory committee for the Yale Law School.

Shefelman was a distinguished member of the bar in Seattle, and for many years until his appointment as a regent he had taught, at eight o'clock in the morning, a course on legal ethics to third-year law students at the University of Washington. I was to learn later that he was a multifaceted civic leader and participant in many causes for the betterment of Seattle and the state of Washington as well as the university. At the time of our first meeting in Ann Arbor in October 1957, he was beginning a two-week trip across the United States to interview several persons under consideration for the Washington presidency.

In November he returned to Ann Arbor for a more extended and leisurely conversation. Subsequently, Betty and I were asked to visit Seattle on January 17 and 18, 1958, to meet the regents, to see the university and its handsome campus, and to visit the beautiful president's residence high on a hill overlooking Lake Washington and the Cascade Mountains. On January 25, 1958, Shefelman again came to Ann Arbor to see Betty and me and to present an informal offer of the presidency, which I informally accepted. These activities led to my acceptance of the formal action of the Board of Regents on January 29, 1958, appointing me President of the University of Washington effective August 1, 1958.

During the next several months I became concerned by the paucity of administrators for academic matters at the top level at Washington. My predecessor as president, Dr. Henry Schmitz, had only one experienced staff associate in his office to aid him in handling the entire range of faculty affairs and the academic instructional program for students. Even that experienced associate, Vice-President H. P. Everest, was destined to retire and, in effect, disappear from the university scene before my actual arrival in Seattle as incoming president in August.

On May 5, I therefore wrote a letter to Mr. Shefelman, as the president of the Board of Regents, expressing the need I felt to have concurrent with my arrival in Seattle an aide especially on the side of academic affairs. I preferred one whose soundness of judgment, understanding of educational matters, administrative competence, and ability in human relations were already known to me.

Fortunately, I knew such a person, Dr. Frederick Patton Thieme, then at the University of Michigan, and I recommended him for the position of Assistant to the President. Born in Seattle in 1914, Thieme had attended grammar and high school there. From 1932 to 1936 he was a student at the University of Washington, obtaining the A.B. degree in 1936. An avid skier as a boy, he persuaded the university to establish a ski team, and for two years was its first captain.

After receiving his baccalaureate degree at Washington in 1936, Thieme was employed over a seven-year span by several manufacturing firms. In 1943, during World War II, he received a commission in the Navy, serving most of the time until February 1946 as officer in charge of Navy Aviation Ordnance for the South Pacific Command. It was his exposure to the native South Pacific islanders and their cultures that aroused his interest especially in physical anthropology and in the possibility of entering the academic profession. After his release from the Navy in 1946, he immediately entered Columbia University, obtaining his Ph.D. in physical anthropology in 1950.

His talents were quickly recognized, and already in 1949 he had been appointed an instructor in anthropology at the University of Michigan, where his advancement in rank to assistant professor, associate professor, and professor was rapid. On three occasions, in 1952, 1954, and 1957, he was asked to serve as acting chairman of the seventeen-member Department of Anthropology during the absence of the chairman. When the chairman, the original founder of the department, chose to request relief from the responsibility of chairmanship, Thieme was the clear choice to succeed him because of his maturity and the department's respect for his great capacity in teaching and research. Thieme also had the respect of faculty from other disciplines in Arts and Sciences. He had been elected to the College's Curriculum Committee and was an outstanding member. His research interest while still at Columbia had also led him to intellectual contacts with Michigan's schools of Engineering, Medicine, and Dentistry.

Because Thieme's parents had continued their lifelong residence in Seattle and on neighboring Vashon Island, he, his wife, and their children were accustomed to summer visits to the Seattle area. They were happy when the Washington regents approved his appointment as my assistant, effective August 1, 1958. The Fred Thieme family was able to plan their arrival in Seattle by that date.

By the end of June 1958, the Odegaard family had arranged to ship to Seattle the clothing, books, household supplies, and furniture we wished to retain. Early in July, Betty and I, with our fifteen-year-old daughter Mary Ann, in a heavily loaded Ford station wagon, began a journey through the South and West to Los Angeles, and then up the Pacific Coast, arriving in Seattle at the beginning of August.

There was one unexpected interruption in our travel schedule when we reached Los Angeles. There, in mid-July, I received a telephone call from Seattle asking me to leave my wife and daughter in a pleasant motel and fly to Seattle for an emergency meeting with the regents concerning the status of the president's residence. There I learned that the regents had received a very negative analysis of the aging plumbing, wiring, heating, and air circulation systems of this private residence that had been built in 1907 for Mr. and Mrs. Edwin Gardner Ames and her parents, Mr. and Mrs. William Walker. The property was presented to the University in the early 1930s and had been the president's residence since then. The technical utilities of the house, dating from 1907 in essence, had never been modernized.

The first alternative proposed at the July meeting was to sell the house and use the proceeds to purchase another one. However, given the spectacular setting of the house and gardens and the appropriateness and scale of its rooms for hosting guests of the university, there was reluctance on my part to abandon the residence.

The regents also wished to hold inaugural ceremonies only three months hence in November.

The final decision reached was to retain the house but defer modernization of its utilities until after the inauguration, when the Odegaards could move temporarily into an apartment for two or three months during which the utilities of the house could be modernized and some spaces could be made more useful. Professor Robert H. Dietz of the College of Architecture supervised the design of improved internal spaces for family, staff, and guests. He also planned the addition, adjacent to the dining room, of a sun porch which would give easy access to the rear garden and its wonderful view. The Ames house thus became an even more friendly and attractive environment for the president's family and for the reception of faculty, staff, students, friends, and visitors to the University of Washington.

An Academic
Presidential Initiative:
Study the
Freshman Year

IN MY OWN FIRST YEAR AT THE UNIVERSITY OF WASH-
ington, I was almost immediately faced with the realization that
far-reaching changes appeared necessary in perhaps the most basic
of academic matters—a student's beginning year on campus. "The
freshman year is the port of entry into an increasingly large collection of educational programs," I wrote in December 1958. As
the array of specializations appropriate to an institution that also
cultivated the upper reaches of higher learning widened, the probability increased dramatically that freshmen would become bewil-
dered and confused by what confronted them. Although a large
measure of responsibility for making an intelligent choice among
courses always rested with the student, there remained the question of what role the faculty should play in assisting and counseling students.

On the horizon was the prospect of a huge growth in enrollment. In 1956 over 123,000 students were attending public high
schools in the state, with predictions of twice that number by 1970.

In August 1958, I prepared a statement for the Board of Regents, subsequently circulated to faculty and staff, analyzing budget and building needs for the next biennium. I pointed out: "The University is a teaching institution and thanks to the change in birth rate there is a treasury of more and more young men and women to be taught. The consequent increases in enrollment have to be met by planned increases in staff, services, and plant, the funds for which must be found."

To whom could I turn for a review of this complicated matter? Thanks to the earlier actions of Business Manager Ernest Conrad, as I will discuss in the following chapter, I had inherited a number of competent administrative colleagues who handled the business and financial affairs of the university. But I myself, at that time still new to Washington, had not yet identified a single academic person already established on the campus who had the wide-ranging experience to make a judgment about all the diverse problems presented by the freshman year.

I therefore appointed a special ad hoc Committee to Study the Freshman Year consisting of Professor Solomon Katz, History, as chairman, and six members: Professor Kermit O. Hanson, Accounting; W. Ryland Hill, Electrical Engineering; Glenn H. Leggett, English; John B. McDiarmid, Classics; Herschel L. Roman, Botany; and Edward L. Ullman, Geography. I asked this committee to consider such questions as:

ᔕ Can the curriculum for the freshman year be simplified or made to appear less complex than is now the case?

ᔕ Is the diversity as great as it appears to be in the catalog listing?

ᔕ What can be done in the way of counseling?

ᔕ What about the procedures for transferring from one college to another to be used by students who feel miscast in their first choice?

In early April 1959 this committee submitted a progress report describing four problem areas of the freshman year—admissions, advising, registration, and curriculum—and suggesting that most of the difficulty arose "not from a lack of machinery but from a lack of a clearly defined and vigorously executed educational policy, and from a lack of easy communication between departments and colleges of the University."

Back in January 1959, seeking more communication between University of Washington faculty members and the teachers from the state's high schools, I had suggested that representatives from the schools meet with university representatives for an exchange of information and opinions. The result was a Principals' Conference held in late April on the university campus, attended by about 125 high school officers and teachers and 50 university representatives. Frederick Thieme, by then the designated University of Washington Provost, in a keynote address based on some of the preliminary findings of the Committee, suggested that it was the responsibility of the university to use the knowledge and experience of high school people to help determine its admission and advising policies, and that it should, in turn, make available to the high schools information about the faculty's perception of the characteristics of the university's students.

Dr. Thieme reported, as a further step toward cooperation with the schools, the appointment of Harold A. Adams as Director of Admissions, thereby making that one office responsible for representing the university and its requirements to the high schools and their student applicants for admission. This was followed also by a description of the various forms of financial aid for students at the university level: scholarships, student loans, and part-time employment.

The conference then turned to discussion of challenges to exceptional students such as honors programs in high schools and at the university level. This was followed by a lengthy session in which the high school representatives were asked to report frankly the comments they had heard from former students about their University of Washington experiences. Before the conference closed, the high school and university representatives were already discussing plans for another meeting the following year.

On February 25, 1960, the members of the Committee to Study the Freshman Year submitted to me a progress report on the issue of undergraduate admissions. Fortunately, they had been able to use results of a recent investigation reported by Professor Paul Horst, Department of Psychology, in which he evaluated the relative success of students in college by comparing their grades with those they had received in high school. Scholastic aptitude was ordinarily measured by the high school grade-point average (GPA). The requirement of a minimal high school GPA was intended to mark the level of scholastic aptitude above which students are likely to succeed at the university and below which they are likely to fail. In most colleges of the University of Washington the minimum high school GPA required for admission was 2.00. For this requirement to be considered effective, most students who met it should subsequently achieve passing grades at the university.

In Horst's study of 5,060 freshmen who entered the University of Washington in 1953 and 1954, he found that 67 percent of those who entered with a high school GPA of 2.00, and 51 percent of those who entered with a GPA of 2.40, failed to achieve a passing GPA of 2.00 at the university.

The technical adviser to the Committee, Robert Guild, also investigated the grades received in the first three quarters of residence by 1,000 freshmen who had entered the university in autumn 1958. He found that the percentage of failures among students with an entering GPA of 2.00 to 2.50 was even higher. He found, further, that 60 percent of the freshmen who entered with a high school GPA of less than 2.50 were on probation at least once during their first three quarters of residence and that the same percentage withdrew from the university before the beginning of their fourth quarter. From these facts it was clear that the minimum grade-point average for admission should be raised to at least 2.50 if the university was going to admit students with an approximately even chance of successful study. The Committee recommended, therefore, that the minimum GPA required for admission should be 2.50.

The Freshman Year Committee also noted that the College of Education and the College of Engineering had slightly higher GPA admission requirements than the other colleges of the university, but found that this difference had little effect on the quality of performance of students admitted to the university. Such lack of uniformity created confusion among entering students, and in the admissions procedures generally. The Committee thus recommended that there be a single minimum freshman GPA admission requirement for the whole university.

The Committee also stated that the requirement of a solid preparation in academic subjects for admission was intended to ensure that students would have the intellectual background and discipline needed for higher education. Since it is on these subjects that success at the university largely depends, the grade-point requirement should be based on them alone, emphasizing to a candidate for admission the importance of a sound and extensive preparation in such subjects. The specific subject requirements were set up only in part to ensure the student's preparation for his or her major field of study. The university was also concerned that its graduates have breadth of intellectual experience and outlook. All colleges of the university recognized in their curricula the need for such breadth, and required it for their degrees. The colleges might properly apply this requirement to all candidates for admission, and regard it as valid whether or not it had any demonstrable effect on the student's performance in his major subject.

Some differences in preparation might be justified, but the Committee questioned the need for such a range of diversity as existed in the subject requirements adopted by the colleges for 1961. It therefore recommended the following subject pattern for admission to all colleges of the University of Washington:

English   3 units
Foreign language   2 units

Mathematics	2 units
Laboratory science	1 unit
Social science	2 units
Academic electives	2 units from the above subjects
Free electives	4 units from the above subjects or from other subjects accepted by an accredited high school for its graduation diploma.

The Committee then appended an extended commentary on the possible impact of the recommended changes. They had clearly raised important issues as to admission and curriculum affecting the operations of nine colleges or schools of the university: Architecture, Arts and Sciences, Business Administration, Education, Engineering, Fisheries, Forestry, Nursing, and Pharmacy. Their deans, chief administrative assistants, and the chairmen of their curriculum committees were interested parties, as were also such faculty standing committees as the Arts and Sciences College Council, the Senate Junior College Committee, the Senate Committee on Admissions, the Senate Committee on Educational Policy, and the Board of Admissions. If the Freshman Year Committee was going to have any effect on the admission and teaching of students, it would somehow have to present its reforming program to those diverse faculty groups for joint discussion and hopefully gain their concurrence.

Fortunately, while I was wondering how to bring these separated groups together in a felicitous environment which would encourage friendly exchange among hitherto disparate faculty members, Dean Gordon Marckworth of the College of Forestry asked me to accompany him to see his college's Pack Forest settlement in a beautiful forested area below the rocky escarpment of Mount Rainier. His college had established these facilities to provide instruction to students of forestry in the summer months and sometimes during spring quarter. There were seven two-room cab-

ins for students, each containing one room equipped with three upper and lower bunk beds, and a second room provided with study
tables, chairs, and a fireplace. Simple washing, bathing, and sani-
tary facilities were available in the nearby washhouse.

There were also four small houses for the dean and three teachers from the Forestry faculty. Meals for faculty and students, and
occasionally other groups, were prepared in a separate kitchen
adjoining a common dining hall, the cooks generally recruited
from friendly neighbors near Pack Forest. Pack Hall, a rustic meeting room heated by a huge fireplace, could easily accommodate
over a hundred persons for presentations and discussion.

I was worried by the tendency toward isolation among the
many schools of the university admitting freshmen, and the absence of evidence of much interchange between them. This was
markedly different from the Freshman Year Committee's hope for
collaboration on both admissions and curriculum across the whole
campus. Pack Forest's combination of a two-hour drive through
spectacular scenery, leading ultimately to some trivial but shared
personal discomfort, particularly for those persons sleeping in the
multiperson bunkhouses, indeed encouraged the opening up of
friendly conversation—as fellow sufferers—among faculty members who had previously been relative strangers to one another. Indeed, some irreverent faculty members called the accommodations
at Pack Forest "Andersonville West," alluding to the notorious Civil
War prison in Georgia.

About ninety members of the faculty met for discussion with
the Freshman Year Committee and the university's principal academic officers on the afternoon and evening of March 16, 1960, and
on the morning of the next day. Their conversations led to acceptance of 2.50 as the minimum grade-point average for admission
of undergraduates. It led also to acceptance of the Committee's
recommended pattern of subjects to be taught in high school as
preparation for admission to all of the University of Washington's
undergraduate schools. The consolidation of the several admis-

sions offices at the university into one overall office for all under-graduates, placed under a capable single director and a consolidated Board of Admissions, was a further step forward attributable to the influence of the Freshman Year Committee under the excellent leadership of Professor Sol Katz.

Chief Administrator of the University of Washington: Broad Goals and Daily Tasks

MY YEARS IN SEATTLE AS PRESIDENT FROM 1958 TO 1973 were stimulating and happy ones. As president of a state university one incurs responsibilities toward a number of constituencies: the faculty, the staff, the students, the alumni, the governor and legislature, professional associations, the business community, the schools, and the general public. But I also believed that the president has an obligation to provide leadership in shaping the academic character of the institution. In part this is exercised by his influence on the kinds of persons appointed to posts as principal academic administrators, who in turn influence the character of departmental leadership.

The president can also exercise academic leadership with regard to the evolution of the research and teaching functions of the university by the power of questioning, by posing issues of policy to committees and study groups, and by his influence on the administrative structures in the institution. The established academic administrative structures, faculties, and departments, if under capable leaders, are likely to handle well the internal business of these units. The hazard is that those new challenges to the institutional and research programs of the university that do not fit the established administrative pigeonholes will fall through the cracks unless someone is watching for them, is pushing for lateral communication, and is initiating flexible catchment administrative structures.

There is obviously much business to be cared for in a university: buildings must be provided and heated; funds collected, budgeted, and spent; faculty and staff recruited and paid; students enrolled; degrees granted. The president is ultimately responsible for these functions, but I cannot imagine being a president without also being involved in concerns for the particular business of the university—learning and teaching. On this business the president has a unique perspective that comes from his opportunity to acquire an overview of the whole scene, the universe of the university. Challenging, yes. Impossible, maybe. But who has better access to it? Why not try, by using the university as a school, to learn as much as one can from all these surrounding experts? What better way is there to continue the pursuit of a liberal education? And what better way to make one continue to be humble about one's own attainments, to make one realize how much there is to know about this fascinating world and how many mysteries still challenge us?

As I wrote in the fall of 1958 during my first month on the job:

The University must do more than dispense inherited knowledge. It must play an active role in amassing and advancing knowledge about an expanding universe from the inside of the atom to the outer galaxies. The natural world of these physical entities is shared by men of many cultures, jostling one another all over the globe, and in need of understanding and knowing about one another. Sputniks overhead, radioactive dust floating by, and the Marines in Lebanon remind us of the enormous challenge to us here in the state of Washington to learn about the world which surrounds us. If the University is to teach its students about the tomorrow in which they will live, it must be an active center of research with staff and facilities required to take part in this great adventure of the mind. This questing activity must pervade the University so that it is truly a teaching and research institution.

One of my first tasks as president of the University of Washington was to make a quick assessment of the manning of the central administrative offices directly below the president and separate from the deans of the schools and colleges. Before my arrival in Seattle in 1958, fiscal and business affairs of the university had been under the management of Nelson A. Wahlstrom, Comptroller and Treasurer, and his principal assistant, Ernest M. Conrad, Business Manager. They had in place a remarkable array of talent able to assist them and the president in dealing with a variety of subsets of the university's business.

However, it transpired that by January 1960, Mr. Wahlstrom was destined to leave for an important post in Washington, D.C., as executive director of the Committee on Governmental Relations of the National Association of College and University Business Officers. Fortunately he would leave at the university Ernest Conrad as a very effective Vice President for Business and Finance, who would continue as a distinguished figure in that role throughout my years as president and until his own retirement in 1974. It was Conrad who was primarily responsible for recruiting the remarkable group of officers I found in 1958 already engaged in handling a wide variety of business affairs. Another important figure for the university's business was Genevieve Michel, assistant to Ernest Conrad. She had no line responsibilities, but worked closely with all the business department heads to ensure coordination in their efforts. During legislative sessions she followed bills introduced to the Washington State Legislature which might have an impact on the university's operations. Business affairs were obviously in competent hands when I arrived. I also had the good fortune to inherit an excellent personal secretary, the long-serving Helen E. Hoagland.

Notably absent at the top administrative level in 1958 was a group of academic officers comparable to the top business officers to whom, as a new president, I could turn for assistance—positions above the level of the deans and directors of the university's schools and colleges but charged with responsibilities in support of the intellectual and academic purposes of the institution. What was indeed evident to me was the great diversity of intellectual matters which had become the object of interest to members of the Washington faculty. Many had reacted to the imperative for research and the more precise definition of subjects of instruction for students.

This situation was reflected in the subject matter and skills already available in the remarkable range of schools and colleges: the College of Architecture and Urban Planning, the School of Art, the College of Arts and Sciences, the College of Business Administration, the School of Communications, the School of Dentistry, the School of Drama, the College of Education, the College of Engineering, the College of Fisheries, the College of Forestry, the Graduate School, the School of Law, the School of Librarianship, the School of Medicine, the School of Mineral Engineering, the School of Music, the School of Nursing, the College of Pharmacy, the School of Physical and Health Education, and the School of Social Work.

The top officers of these diverse academic units, whether designated deans, directors, or executive officers, had become accustomed in the recent past to exercising substantial independence in the management of the affairs of their units. They had been exposed to little intervention from either the former president or the vice-president, who had already retired in July before my arrival in August 1958. They had left no senior officers to assist an incoming president in dealing with the academic aspects of the University of Washington. It was this situation which made so necessary my request to the regents to bring Frederick Thieme to Seattle as my principal assistant for academic affairs.

Thieme's role in this regard was recognized in 1959 under the title of Provost. By 1961 he was assisted by a professor of English, Glenn Leggett, as Vice Provost. When Thieme was designated Vice President in 1964, Leggett was named Provost, and a professor of geography, Marion Marts, was named Vice Provost. When Leggett left the university in 1966 to accept the presidency of Grinnell College in Iowa, he was replaced as Provost by Solomon Katz, professor of history, who in the preceding years had served as Dean of the College of Arts and Sciences.

A major readjustment occurred again in 1968 when Thieme left to become president of the University of Colorado at Boulder. Katz replaced him as Executive Vice President for Academic Affairs and Provost. In 1969, Dr. John Hogness was designated Executive Vice President, Director of the Health Sciences Center, and Chairman of the Board of Health Sciences. In 1971, Philip W. Cartwright, a professor of economics, was appointed Executive Vice President.

Another person who became an important member of the president's staff with regard to public relations as well as academic matters was Robert G. Waldo, who, when I came in 1958, was Dean of Men under Dean of Students Donald K. Anderson. I soon recognized Waldo's many talents as a negotiator both with other educational institutions and with legislators and government staffs. Subsequently I brought him into my office, first in 1962 as Assistant to the President, then in 1963 as Director of Planning and Development, and, in 1965 and thereafter, until the end of my presidency in 1973, as Vice President for University Relations.

We soon recruited in the ensuing years a coterie of subordinate officers to work between the president and vice presidents on the one hand and the deans of the schools and colleges on the other, to focus in particular on academic and intellectual matters. From my experience at the University of Michigan, I had recognized the need of a president to have a group of intellectually oriented assistants capable of monitoring and encouraging interaction about ideas among the deans and faculty members of the separate schools and colleges which might then lead to useful joint intellectual ventures and exchanges. I was convinced that the intellectual activity of a university certainly deserves as much attention from a president and his staff as its business affairs receive.

From the very beginning of my tenure, a meeting was scheduled each workday morning from 8:30 to 9:00 in the Regents'

Room of the Administration Building. Those attending this so-called cabinet were Odegaard, Thieme, Wahlstrom, Conrad, Helen Hoagland, and Neil Hines (who handled documentation and publicity). As the occasion warranted, these persons could be joined by particular officers for fiscal and business affairs as well as for academic matters. This early morning meeting was used for a quick update on matters immediately under review by members of the central staff of the university administration. It was accompanied once a week by a longer meeting for updates and discussion of academic as well as business issues.

I initially became acquainted with most of the deans during a brief talk in my office, but I made a special effort over time to meet each dean in his or her own office and school environment, where he or she could present me with a more multidimensional view of the school's educational program. I can still remember my exhausting tour of the relatively new Medical School laboratories and classrooms led by its dedicated and long-legged dean, George Aagaard. I also began a process, when I found an hour or two of unscheduled time on my calendar, of calling a department chairman in one or another school of the university to see if he or she had some free time for a conversation with me about the department and a tour of its facilities.

I soon learned also that the regents, when rapid coverage of their meeting's agenda permitted a postlude, greatly enjoyed an opportunity to meet for informal conversation with the dean of a school or the chairman of a department within the latter's own teaching and learning environment. In retrospect, I believe that the easy, informal interchange between the regents and the faculty members that developed quickly was encouraged by the fact that by long-established statutory tradition the Board of Regents during my fifteen years of service as president consisted of only seven members, a number small enough to encourage an easy congeniality among the regents themselves and also with the faculty deans or chairmen with whom they shared these informal sessions.

The University
and Higher
Education in
Washington State

I SOON CAME TO REALIZE THAT I COULD NOT EFFEC-
tively manage my responsibilities to the university without concern
for the larger context of Washington State. Projections of enrollment trends made soon after my arrival in 1958 showed that, if there
were no changes in the structure of higher education in the state,
the University of Washington on a business-as-usual basis could
face in a few years an increase in enrollment from the 16,000 level
to well over 50,000. This probability made imperative a redefinition
of the state's responsibility for higher education for all students,
university and nonuniversity.

The role of the university could not be clarified, I was convinced, without clarifying the roles of the other postsecondary
institutions. I therefore felt an obligation to step forward to seek
consultation and cooperation with the heads of the other higher
institutions in the state. I first sought communication with the
president of the institution whose program was most like that at
the University of Washington—namely, Washington State University at Pullman. We then sought meetings with the presidents of the

three state colleges whose institutions had expanded their offerings after World War II to include, in addition to teacher training, a program for undergraduates in liberal arts and sciences and some master's degree programs. The five of us then met in my home with the administrative heads of the eleven junior colleges in the state which were legally defined as extended secondary institutions administratively responsible to the superintendent of schools in the school district in which the college was located. Through collaborative effort we prepared a document on criteria and procedures for the establishment of additional community colleges for the state.

When it became evident that there were serious deficiencies stemming from the dependence of the community colleges upon the school districts, the presidents of the five senior institutions publicly recommended the creation of a new statewide structure for community colleges. In 1967, the Legislature responded by dividing the entire state into twenty-two community-college districts under a statewide board, with each district having its own local board responsible for one or more campuses. In addition to the provision of a two-year academic-transfer program for students desiring to continue their education at a four-year college or university, there was increased emphasis on the provision of vocational and technical courses and on general education in the community colleges.

Meanwhile, the five presidents had recommended the establishment of a new state college in the southwestern portion of the state, authorized by the Legislature in 1967 as Evergreen State College, and intended to improve regional access to four-year institutions in the state.

There thus emerged for the state a tripartite structure for higher education: the two state universities; the four state colleges; and twenty-two community-college-district institutions. There was some measure of success in achieving a sharp distinction of educational functions among the three types of institutions and in altering the pattern of distribution of students by level among the institutions. It was possible to develop a sharper focus on the University of Washington as a research-oriented institution carrying a higher proportion of graduate and advanced professional students and more upper-division undergraduates than lower-division students. The regional colleges and the community colleges absorbed a greater proportion of students at the lower levels, and it was possible by the early 1970s to stabilize the enrollment at the University of Washington around the 35,000 level. It was gratifying to me as a participant in this effort to hear the leading expert on statewide coordination of higher education express the opinion that the Council of Presidents in Washington had carried voluntary coordination further than it had been carried in any other state of the union.

The day came, however, when problems began to emerge that could not be resolved by voluntary agreement among the institutions. As a member of the Temporary Advisory Council on Higher Education established by the Legislature, I supported a recommendation for the creation by the Legislature of a formal statewide Council on Higher Education, whose voting members would be nine public citizens approved by the governor.

The problems facing higher education still abound. I do not think that one institution in our society can prosper long, however devoted its immediate following may be, without the exercise of a general concern for the quality, relevance to societal needs, and effectiveness of the whole body on higher education.

The mood in which I undertook the challenge of the presidency of the University of Washington is reflected in the conclusion of my inaugural remarks in 1958. I had reread, shortly before, *The Aims of Education* by Alfred North Whitehead, the distinguished philosopher whom I had come to know in my years at Harvard as a teacher and friend. Through these contacts I had become aware of his firm belief in the use of reason, however blunted it might be, before the complexities of this world, and of his conviction that the universities had to be the guardians and caretakers of this intellectual civilization.

In *The Aims of Education*, Professor Whitehead said: "The

Aegean Coastline had its chance and made use of it; Italy had its chance and made use of it; France, England, Germany had their chance and made use of it. Today the Eastern American states have their chance. What use will they make of it? That question has two answers. Once Babylon had its chance, and produced the Tower of Babel. The University of Paris fashioned the intellect of the Middle Ages."

In my inaugural address I noted:

Professor Whitehead voyaged far in his own lifetime. He liked adventures in living as well as in ideas. His historical sense taught him how the torch of learning had passed from Greece to Rome to Paris to modern Germany, and England, and to the Eastern states of the United States. He himself helped in this westward pilgrimage of learning by moving from the old Cambridge in England to the new Cambridge in Massachusetts. If he were alive today, pondering on these matters a quarter century later, he would not have been surprised, I believe, by the thought that the Western states might have their chance too. . . .

We are all in this world together, and it is imperative that the torches of learning be held aloft and tended in many places. In purely national terms it is not enough to have a handful of great universities for a country of 175,000,000, and those mostly in the East. If this intellectual civilization that Whitehead prized is to survive and prosper in these United States, there must be a string of creative, I repeat, creative universities from East to West and North to South. The Western states must do their part in accepting and building nothing but the best. . . .

All of us, Eastern and Western, in and out of universities, must work in the hope that the American people will be enabled to escape the curse that now threatens modern man, the awesome great sentence that was noted by Professor Whitehead in the following words: "In the conditions of modern life the rule is absolute, the race which does not value trained intelligence is doomed. Not all your heroism, not all your social charm, not all your wit, not all your victories on land or at sea, can move back the finger of fate. To-day we maintain ourselves. To-morrow science will have moved forward yet one more step, and there will be no appeal from the judgment which will then be pronounced on the uneducated."

We must in the Western states take up still more the slack and not rely as much as in the past on what the Eastern states have provided if we are to give our sons and daughters their just due and to enable them and us to acquit ourselves of our fair share of responsibility in preventing all America from receding into the accursed land of the uneducated.

It was to such a task that I dedicated myself at the University of Washington.

A Season
of Discontent and
the Establishment
of a Black Studies
Program

THE HOPES AND EXPECTATIONS OF THE EARLY 1960S
created an atmosphere of exhilaration as well as an atmosphere of
tension on the University of Washington campus and throughout
the country. In 1965 the university admitted 2,222 more students
than it had in the previous year, the largest increase faced by the
university in its entire history, except for the post-World War II
years. Enrollment projections called for 32,400 students by 1970,
double the student population of 1958.

If the general public came to place more and more of the responsibility for mankind's future upon the university, the institution itself was setting ambitious goals that challenged the resources
and imagination of its faculty, administration, and staff. In 1964 I
reported to the faculty: "The continuing redefinition of the role of
the university in a changing society—and accordingly, the number, level, and kind of students to be admitted to it—requires your
interest not only in terms of the internal analysis of the relationship
of your specialized field to the larger university but in terms of the

total context of post-high school education into which the University fits."

"Even then," I concluded, "unless there is developed a larger public consensus on a broad and comprehensive educational philosophy and policy for higher education, the separate parts of post-high school education, including the University, will have difficulty in carrying out their roles."

At the meeting of the Faculty Senate on April 15, 1965, I presented a special report entitled "The Season of Discontent." I affirmed that a feeling of discontent had evolved among Washington students, which obviously had expressed itself in matters of civil and political rights. Some highly dissident students expected their liberties to be restricted, but they were finding it rather difficult to establish such a case. We had made no regulations against participation in political demonstrations; we had not been interfering with free expression on the campus.

This season of discontent covered a broader palette than political and civil liberties, involving questions that included, in large measure, a critical analysis of education per se. It had to do, indeed, with the nature of the educational experience students in this and other institutions were having. I personally thought there was a fair amount of exaggeration in the comments of dissenters on the sterility of the educational process on campus, the inhumanity of the UW, the absence of personal warmth.

In any case, these charges could hardly be directed solely at the president of a university, cast in a role of personal father-confessor to all students. It is not possible to exclude the faculty from considerations involving students, since the human relationships that exist on campus are largely between professors and their students. Nothing contributes more to the students' feeling of a sense of humanness about a university than a high level of faculty concern for them as individuals. Faculty members, it is true, may become so preoccupied with the processes of their own learning, their own research, that they may devote little time to teaching and conversation with students.

We had seen the development of greater flexibility of instruction in the form of new educational opportunities such as the honors program, in which various members of the faculty were involved. Consequently, I did not wish to convey the idea that we needed a "panic" operation to restore balance in our program because of any alleged "flight from teaching."

Students are our perennial responsibility. Had we done all that we should do? My own conviction was that we needed to go beyond chance personal contact between teacher and student to seek an organized and institutionalized way to listen to students. I saw no reason why we should not bring them into more contact with professors and advisers. The administrative offices of the university were already working with planning committees to produce a more humane environment for faculty and students in new and remodeled buildings. And of course major efforts were made to increase the size of the faculty and support system in response to the growing enrollment.

We heard a great deal about office hours and having professors more available. But all of this, it seemed to me, had to go along with something else which the younger generation sooner or later must learn. One cannot escape, in this life, the requirement of discipline—discipline in the sense of subjection to demands for standards of performance. Sooner or later, the university would have to be recognized by students as a disciplined and disciplining intellectual institution. We should not permit sentimentality to undermine the demand for quality in their university work.

Sometime later, in the spring of 1968, while I was pondering this matter, my secretary came to my office to tell me that several black students had appeared in the waiting room, asking to see me. It then transpired that there were also some other black students in the outer hall, too many for the group to fit into my small personal office space. My secretary then told a group, about ten in all, to go into the Regents' Room and seat themselves around the regents' table.

When I entered the room I sat down in the one empty chair at the end of the table. Before I could speak, a man near the other end of the table spoke up in a loud voice: "The only reason you are meeting with us is because you are scared, you are scared, you are scared!" I immediately reacted with the silent thought that for the moment I was indeed a bit scared, but so was he—even more so! This exposure led to some ensuing discussion between me and E. J. Brisker, the president of the Black Student Union. I concluded rather quickly that the faculty themselves should be given the opportunity to hear the case Brisker and his colleagues could present for greater contact with the university faculty. I became impressed by Brisker's desire for reasonable discussion with the faculty, and suggested to him that he prepare a report to present to the Faculty Senate. He did so in the following statement at the Senate meeting of May 23, 1968:

Remarks Addressed to the Senate by the President of the Black Student Union

We, the representatives of the BLACK STUDENT UNION, wish to thank the Faculty Senate for their invitation. We've approached this presentation with a strong sense of the need for change in the present University's educational structure.

Specifically, we would like the support of the Faculty Senate in three key areas. One, in the area of recruitment of non-white students. Two, the development of programs, i.e., remedial and tutorial, that will aid newly recruited students in making the difficult transition to university life. Three, the development of a Black Studies Curriculum which will enable *both non-white and white* students to learn about the culture and life style of such groups as Afro-American, Mexi-American, and Indian-American peoples.

The setting up of a Black Studies Curriculum would offer the University an exciting educational challenge, a challenge to set up a course of studies that would attract scholars and philosophers from all over the world.

The precedent for a course of studies that focuses on diverse cultures has already been made. Two examples rush quickly to mind. One, the University of Washington presently has Scandinavian studies; two, the University also has Far Eastern studies.

Amid all the recent "sound and fury" the Black Student Union feels that certain aspects of our demands have been interpreted incorrectly. In a certain sense, the Black Student Union's linguistic approach was at fault. Several examples come to mind. One, we used the word "demand" when it was probably better to use the word "suggest." The use of the word demand gave a distorted image of the Black Student Union as a group of fanatic, rabble-rousing people. Actually, our group was attempting to offer concrete, positive solutions to the problems that threaten to perpetuate the cancer of racism.

A second example was our use of the words "direct and control." Many sincere white and non-white people interpret the words to mean that we were trying to take power away from Dr. Odegaard, to destroy the prestige of a great University, and to tell a brilliant and distinguished faculty what to teach and how to teach it. We want to make it crystal clear that while we want to participate vigorously in all aspects of the program, we are not asking for control. Many people have misunderstood this.

At this point we must try to clarify our position. One, we recognize that the University should and must direct the activities of the University of Washington. Two, we recognize that Dr. Odegaard has made some attempts to work for a more humane University community. Three, we recognize that concerned students, faculty, and administration must come together to find ways to cure racism.

Realizing that we need the resources and energy of students, faculty and administrators, the BSU asks: 1) that the Faculty Senate pass a resolution supporting our demands and 2) that the idea of a Black Studies curriculum be placed on the agenda of the Long Range Planning Committee of each Department of the various Schools and Colleges of the University.

Finally, we must tell the Senate about another human problem. The Black Student Union does not have many members. We are full time students and we are trying to help this University change and become a greater University. We find that this has taken an enormous amount of our time. We have been required to attend many faculty and administrative meetings, too many committee meetings, for the good of our studies. Some members of the Black Student Union want to go to graduate school, but if they make C's they cannot get in. Thus, we ask you to understand our situation; to give us a chance to study while you shoulder some of the burdens of making the necessary changes. We are worried about our academic futures, but we are sacrificing them in order to help this University grow greater. Our academic problems this term are acute. We ask you to understand.

We are pleased and honored by your invitation and we hope that our presentation *will be the start* of positive communication and interaction between the BSU and the Faculty Senate.

E. J. BRISKER
President, Black Student Union

The reasoned approach which Brisker used on behalf of the black students opened the door to communications and a cooperative spirit between them and the university faculty and administrators. The thoughtful and carefully prepared proposals made by Brisker and his student associates quickly evoked favorable responses from the Faculty Council on Academic Standards. The latter endorsed the principle of consultation with the Black Student Union concerning decisions, plans, and programs affecting the lives of black students and efforts to aid their recruitment and entry into the student body at the university.

It should be noted that Brisker asked for Faculty Senate support in developing a Black Studies Program to attract and recruit both white and non-white students. He averred that non-white students needed such courses so that they could know more about their heritage, and also develop a cultural base as a necessary foundation for interaction with people of other cultures. White students also needed such courses in order to interact in positive ways with an 80 percent non-white world. It should be noted that faculty members, both white and a growing number of color, who could teach such courses had been appearing at the University of Washington increasingly in recent years.

Fortunately, the Senate's Faculty Council on Academic Standards under the leadership of its chairman, Professor Morton

David, in the three weeks before Brisker presented his report to the Senate, had led his Senate Committee in a review of concerns and had reached the conclusion that the current system was too slowly responsive to student needs, and that by opening channels of faculty-student communication on all levels, faculty and students could profit from the experience and turn frustration into constructive action. The Council concluded that the basic demands of the Black Student Union, when interpreted so as not to impair the responsibility of the university to maintain its ultimate control, were reasonable and could enrich considerably the life of the University of Washington as a whole.

The Faculty Council also agreed to increase a specified number of non-whites for admission to the university by September and to facilitate tutoring of them. The Council expressed the belief that a program of Black Studies would increase black student pride in their own cultural backgrounds. The Council also expressed support for efforts to recruit black faculty and administrators.

The report of the Faculty Council on Academic Standards received Senate endorsement by acclamation.

Professor Philip W. Cartwright, Dean of the College of Arts and Sciences, in May 1968 appointed seven professors to serve on a Special Curriculum Committee on Black American Culture with the help of a student advisory group which included among its membership representatives of the Black Student Union and white students.

The Special Curriculum Committee, after careful deliberation, recommended in June 1968 that a Black Studies Program be established at the University of Washington. That program was set up by the end of 1968, and in the following two years analogous programs were established in American Indian Studies, Chicano Studies, and Asian American Studies.

Here was a case in which a number of black students wanted to talk to the university faculty and administrators. They really wanted something that could be accomplished within the univer-

sity framework. Because of their inexperience and lack of understanding of the university, they sometimes asked for things in a way
that could not be granted in the particular form they asked for. But
there were useful things that could be done in their behalf. Hence,
we found ourselves on a constructive course with black students on
this campus, and also with Mexican American, American Indian,
and Asian American students.

A National Phenomenon: Student Disruption on the University Campus, 1969–1970

THE GROWING INTEREST OF STUDENTS IN POLITICAL issues of course raised policy questions regarding the appropriate relationship of the University of Washington to particular forms of action. It had not been necessary to give much thought to such "politicization" in the past, because for at least a couple of decades students had shown little tendency to become involved in national, state, and local politics, however much some might be engaged in campus politics. In times past, students were largely undergraduates ranging in age between eighteen and twenty-one, and it was easy for the idea to develop that those who were in college lived a life apart and entered the active area of citizen politics only after graduation.

Even though the age distribution of students shifted substantially after World War II toward an increased enrollment of older persons, the apathetic mood of the 1950s affected the university population and encouraged the retention of traditional attitudes about the low level of student interest in politics. Those not close to the scene of university life in the 1960s failed to appreciate the

changing mood of students and the consequences of the changing age distribution. The student population was far from fitting
stereotyped notions of the older generation about "college kids."

A quick analysis of the composition of the student body by age
is illuminating. I have in mind the regularly enrolled students pur-
suing degree courses, who in the autumn of 1969 totaled 32,749 persons. Of these, 3 were in their seventies, 32 were in their sixties, 193
were in their fifties, 952 were in their forties, 2,728 were in their thirties, and 16,834 were between twenty-one and twenty-nine years
old: a total of 20,742 were twenty-one or older. Thus at least 63.3
percent of our students, minus a very small number who were for-
eigners, were qualified to vote in this country. (This was, of course,
before the eighteen-year-old vote became law.) Almost two-thirds
of the students were therefore eligible to vote, and thus potentially
someone's constituents.

In the fall of 1969, the kind of student dissent that had emerged
by April 1965 at the University of Washington was spreading, especially among the younger generations of students enrolled in colleges and universities across the country. It was inspired in part by
dissatisfaction among diverse racial and social groups and in part
by growing resistance to the nation's unpopular war against Vietnam. High levels of tension and conflict were being reached, notably in the East at Columbia University in New York, and in the
West at the University of California in Berkeley.

Fortunately, the University of Washington population did not
ultimately reach the level of disruption that occurred on many
campuses, for there was already some history of efforts by administrators, faculty, and students to communicate with one another
on sources of discontent. At least partly, these sources were internal and attributable to stresses and strains within our own institution. But student participation in university committees with
faculty members and administrative officers was under way, and
the regents were also responding to both student and faculty requests for discussion of current issues.

Professor Joseph McCarthy, as dean of the Graduate School, and his faculty associates started discussions with graduate students that led to the creation of an independent body of elected student representatives, the Graduate and Professional Student Senate (GPSS). The deans of the various schools and colleges of the university also reviewed the mechanisms for consultation with their student groups at the school and college level.

But there was no guarantee, of course, that these efforts would discourage the more extreme dissenters or activist revolutionaries who might appear among our students, faculty, or staff, or from off campus, and who might indeed choose to engage in forcible disruption of university activity and in violence against persons, property, and records as part of their attempts to close down the University of Washington. The efforts of extremists to go beyond peaceful demonstrations to violent actions were sometimes deterred by substantial responses by other students, faculty, and administrators to predictable situations. Joint cooperation through the Graduate and Professional Student Senate, the Associated Students of the University of Washington, and the Faculty Senate generally made clear the lack of sympathy most persons on campus had for violent forms of action or expressions of dissent.

In contrast to the peaceful conduct and resolution of the protest by black students in 1968, some other campus demonstrators turned to violence in an incident on February 24, 1969, where individual students were prevented from attending job recruiting interviews for which they had signed up. A militant and organized crowd at the break between classes poured into the lobby and outer office area of the placement center in Loew Hall. Then a noisy mass surged into an interviewing room, pushing the interviewer back toward the wall, overturning and breaking the table behind which he was seated. The university security officer, in view of this behavior, tried to get the interviewer out, and to get him out quickly for his own safety. This was clearly violent disruption.

The next day's *Daily*, the student paper, quoted the leader of the demonstrations as saying that the Loew Hall episode was only practice, that they would go after the ROTC in Savery Hall on March 6. Threats of this sort continued to be uttered each day.

In response to the actions at Loew Hall, the Faculty Senate, in a meeting on February 27, 1969, fully recognized the rights of individuals to assemble and picket reasonably, but resolved that such activities should not interfere with the rights of others. Therefore the Senate supported those regulations that guaranteed free ingress to and egress from any university building, and which ensured the normal functioning and activities of the university community through all of its facilities.

At that meeting of the Faculty Senate, I stated that I could not help but see an analogy between our affairs and those of another country, as I observed these bullyboy tactics. Many years earlier I had been in Germany twice during the period of Nazi control. People tend now to look back at Nazi Germany from the end of the story. We remember the horrors of the concentration camps and of the invading Nazi crimes that swept over Europe. We do not examine how that regime came to possess tyrannical power.

I was reminded of a conversation that occurred in the summer of 1968 when the Executive Committee of the Senate, first under Chairman Evans and then under Chairman Aldrich, held a series of discussions on the problem of student dissent and the disorders on campuses. At one of the meetings, two faculty members were asked to relate their experiences under totalitarian regimes. Professor Hans Neurath described events in Austria before World War II and Professor Konrad Buettner spoke of Germany. The fascinating thing about Professor Buettner's story was that he did not say anything about the Nazi regime after it took over. He confined his remarks to events of the pre-Hitler period which paved the way for Hitler's accession. He said that after Hitler seized power the story was really over. It was what people failed to do earlier to resist his bullyboys and their demonstrations that really explained his access to power. In Germany itself in the mid-thirties I saw the last flickering out of the light of freedom, which had not been tended in the period before Hitler actually took over the government.

If we believe in liberal democracy, there is a point where we too may have to fight back in favor of its principles, when the liberal belief in "let the other fellow have his way" must be carefully considered against his willingness to conduct himself with respect for others. We too may have to insist upon respect for the rule of law as the last protection of the liberties of each person. The law may be imperfect and permit impurities, but parliamentary procedures provide a safer and better course of change than force and threats of force.

There are two parts to this equation. There is the maintenance of the free right of individuals to have their own opinions and to express them, often tested by acceptance of dissent however unpopular. This has certainly been underlined repeatedly in academic committees. But there is also resistance to those who go beyond the expression of dissent and use force and violence to impose their opinions on others. Are we going to underline the other part of the equation? The enforcement of the rule is the best protection for the rights of individuals. In response to force, should we not invoke sanctions against those whose clear intent is to destroy the liberties of others and at the same time the essence of the minority ideal? I was delighted that the Faculty Senate addressed itself directly to this problem and spoke up.

I was not, however, reassured by the change in tactics early in 1970 by some extremists. Our options in the face of their new methods of disruption were narrowed, and we had no recourse but to call for help from all available peacekeeping forces. We proceeded against identified perpetrators of hit-and-run attacks on persons and property on the campus by submitting all relevant information to the King County prosecuting attorney for appropriate action—against students and off-campus persons alike. We hoped that we could manage our own affairs and maintain our sense of solidarity in the face of the emergencies that might arise so that we could continue to present a measure of internal and peaceful control at the University of Washington.

I was deeply distressed by signs in American life of a lack of respect by a growing number of people for the forms of societal decision making in America embodied in procedures built upon the complex of constitutionally protected individual rights, the democratic parliamentary methods for legislative decision making in the name of society at large, the separated powers of the administration and the judiciary, and the supporting mechanisms of the party system. The means by which we reach decisions on environmental decay, racial discrimination, equality of the sexes, foreign policy, or educational change in universities may have as much effect on the ultimate quality of the lives of each and every one of us as the content of the decisions themselves. For these decision-making procedures in our society are themselves impregnated with important human values: they are so designed as to provide protection for the liberties of individuals and at the same time, since man is a social animal, to provide a carefully conceived method of developing wide consensus for the decisions necessary for the attainment of a better society.

As a medievalist who has studied the decay of ancient civilization, the unleashing of brute force in the early Middle Ages, and the centuries-long struggle to create restraints on raw power over individuals and to develop a better social order for all, I know that our American political heritage contains many precious elements, the loss of which, through indifference or assault, will leave us much the poorer. We all know that our system is subject to abuse, both by corruption of its parts and by slowness of reaction to new or newly perceived needs. But, balanced against other possibilities, it is so far superior to the alternatives that we opt at our peril if we reject it instead of using its own inbuilt devices for remedying social conditions. Those who elect to reach for the sword rather than to use our inherited political and legal processes had better be sure of their prophecies as to who tomorrow's victor will be.

After my handling of a troubled time on campus toward the end of 1969 and the beginning of 1970, the members of the Board of Regents and my administrative colleagues urged me to obtain some release from tension by taking a four-week auto trip in Portugal, which began with my departure with my wife from Seattle on February 18, 1970. My colleagues were to encounter stormy problems during my absence about which I learned nothing until my return to Seattle on March 17.

During my absence, there had been a turn on the campus toward more violence. The Black Student Union had demanded that the university administration issue a public statement against all forms of racism, denounce Brigham Young University as a racist institution, and immediately sever all relations with that institution (meaning, in actual effect, to cancel some intercollegiate athletic competitions with BYU).

It had long been the policy of the University of Washington not to discriminate against individuals by reason of race, and to make its facilities available to Americans of all races. Our policy had evolved, as has been indicated above, from the stage of neutrality as to race to a commitment to positive action programs intended to assist minority students in overcoming accumulated social, psychological, and educational barriers to their use of the university. This commitment also included recognition of the need for curricular development so that all students might be aware of the cultural characteristics and contributions of these hitherto segregated minorities within our midst.

Despite the angry responses from some quarters, directed against blacks and against the university for trying to aid them, and despite the fact that certain actions of blacks were not to be condoned, I believed that the University of Washington should not turn away from its dedication to constructive, positive programs of action to alleviate the cancer of race relations in our society.

Events on our campus had made the University of Washington's commitment to remedial action in the direction of equal opportunity for all unpopular in some quarters, but dedication to this goal remained crucial to the salvation of America. I thought that we should not falter in our determination to find ways to assist whites, on the one hand, and minority groups, on the other, to overcome the social and individual consequences of the historic legacy of segregation in our society. I was aware that among blacks there was a segment of extremists prepared to use terroristic tactics and violent means. But when the 1969–70 demonstrations on campus escalated to a violent stage, it was by no means solely a black action.

To resolve the crisis that had flared up during my absence over the use of violence to influence our university's relations with Brigham Young University, I set forth my policies in a statement to the Board of Regents on March 27, 1970:

I believe that the University should endeavor to honor the commitments it has already made to Brigham Young University for intercollegiate athletic events. Individual student athletes who do not wish to participate as a matter of conscience should be free not to participate in the scheduled meets.

The University administration should refrain from the denunciation of Brigham Young University as a racist institution, demanded by the Blacks. As far as future scheduling is concerned, the Department of Sports Programs should include among its considerations the attitudes expressed by students and faculty. If there are a substantial number of students and faculty who do not wish further association with BYU, then this becomes a factor deserving of consideration in making the particular decision as to future scheduling of intercollegiate meets.

The decision to schedule or not to schedule further meets with BYU certainly could be reached on this ground without accepting the proposition that the University of Washington has to be the judge of the merits of one argument over another in the matter of the conflict between religious and civil rights associated with the controversy over BYU because of its Mormon association. The appropriate place for the resolution of this dispute lies elsewhere than in the University of Washington.

The University of Washington should continue unabated in its effort to help, through its own educational programs, the achievement of a society offering equal opportunity to all regardless of racial origins. I hope that most Blacks at least will accept our determination to continue to work with them to open opportunities to them and to develop a society in which Blacks and Whites emerge as fellow Americans sharing in a cultural tradition which has been enriched by the contributions of all parties. I hope that they will accept the reasons why the University has not denounced BYU and has not canceled its current agreements with BYU.

At the same time, I hope that the Whites will accept the course of action presented here as the wisest one possible in this tangled situation and will have some understanding of the Blacks' aspirations and feelings. For either Whites or Blacks to permit these events further to polarize their feelings on the racial issue will only exacerbate an already cancerous situation in our body politic and increase the chances for destruction of American society.

Finally, we cannot and should not ignore the fact that the violence on our campus earlier this month and similar violence directed toward other universities and other types of institutions underline the presence in our society of violent revolutionaries who are willing to go to any length to bring down the institutions and traditional framework of American society. We need to keep viable our established ways for remedying the ills of our society and adapting it to new needs and better visions of a good society. Our own zeal for reformation should continue unabated.

But we must recognize the need to protect our institutions from those who work, not for their correction by peaceable means, but for their destruction by force and violence. We cannot countenance their attacks; we must resist them. The kind of violence against persons and property, the kind of disruption of the normal activities of the University, which marked the violence of the March days must be contained by the University's calling for all the police protection it may need and can obtain from outside.

If similar actions are perpetrated on campus again, we will not hesitate again to ask for help as we did during those March days. Indeed, as I have indicated, I have asked the Governor and Legislature, in association with local authorities, to review the capacities of the agencies of this state to deal with violence and riots whether revolutionaries select as their targets universities, colleges, schools, courts, city halls, public agencies or private enterprises. We must work together to keep America flexible enough to meet new challenges and to improve our society through peaceful, evolutionary political processes. We must, at the same time, work together to contain more effectively the revolutionaries bent on the destruction of our constitutional and democratic system.

The Peace
Movement on
Campus and the
Student Strike,
May 1970

THE ENTRY OF U.S. ARMED FORCES INTO CAMBODIA early in 1970 led to protest demonstrations on many campuses around the United States, including the University of Washington. In the protest at Kent State University, four students were killed by members of the National Guard, and two more students died in the violence that erupted on the campus at Jackson State College in Mississippi. To protest these events, a "strike" by students took place on the University of Washington campus in May 1970, and strikers moved from the campus to march on Interstate 5 to the federal courthouse in downtown Seattle.

I thought it fortunate that the broad majority of leaders and supporters of the Strike Coalition chose to define strike not as closure of the University of Washington, or as recourse to measures of disruption, but as the winning of opportunities to help mobilize the general peace movement. The mature and responsible way the Subcommittee on Grade Amnesty performed its work, and the generous response of the Faculty Senate to its proposals, seemed to me good examples of the positive results of a peaceful and rational pursuit of objectives.

The same could be said of many of the meetings within the academic units of the university, where students and faculty discussed their own approaches to the problem of peace. These activities had been complemented by growing student peace activity in the community and had won wide respect for the maturity and seriousness of our student body, and greater understanding for the peace movement which so many of them represented and supported.

It was therefore both a surprise and a disappointment when I received on May 15, 1970, an open letter from Mr. Block and Mr. Silverman, two leaders of the Strike Coalition. For that letter indicated that the Coalition's leaders were determined once again to turn inward—to raise internal university issues and turn away from the main issue as discerned by the great majority of activist students and faculty, the issue of American policy in Indochina.

The Coalition became a force on the campus precisely because it helped to provide the organization and the forum for discussion and action on the Vietnam issue. But the open letter made it appear that some would make the issue of peace in Indochina simply an instrument for the radical restructuring of the university. I believed that the majority of students would reject that strategy and the narrow political viewpoint it represented, just as they had rejected a notion of strike aimed at disruption, coercion, and closure.

I was also disappointed in the specific proposal from Mr. Block and Mr. Silverman which called for the determination of University of Washington policy by a binding referendum submitted to the faculty, staff, administration, and students on a one-man, one-vote basis. The particular matter on which a referendum was called for was designated in the May 15 open letter as "whether ROTC, Classified Research, the National Guard, and BYU have a place on this campus." Presumably on another day, it could also be proposed that other university matters be decided by such a one-man, one-vote referendum.

The hope was expressed in the open letter that what is called my "answer" would be presented at the noon rally on Tuesday, May 19. The language suggested that the president of the university has the power to refer university decision making to such a referendum. Any such notion is far from the truth. Even if I believed in the validity of this particular method of university decision making—which I do not—I did not have the authority to set aside the complex system of university decision-making procedures based on law, custom, and common sense.

The concept underlying this referendum proposal presupposed that the university is an autonomous, self-determining, self-supporting community, the participants in which have equal rights and equal capacity to decide all matters coming before it by procedures of a populist democracy, by the will of a majority as indicated in a referendum. This concept was totally out of touch with the realities of the case.

The University of Washington is not a total community in and of itself, autonomous, self-determining, and self-supporting. Its community does not constitute a kind of separate state. It is a social institution, charged by the larger society through acts of the Legislature with particular purposes; it is subject to regulation by the larger society through the legislative, executive, and judicial branches of government—regulation which may be loose or tight as these agencies external to the university decide. In short, it is a limited purpose community which must be responsive to the larger society.

The university is a place set aside within society by society to nurture higher learning for that society. Legal authority is vested in the Board of Regents, who are appointed to serve as trustees for the public's interest. While they may delegate, and do delegate, responsibility for actual decision making very widely throughout the institution—depending on the subject—to administrators, faculty, or students, theirs is the ultimate authority.

Under the general direction of the regents, the university is staffed with faculty, an experienced group of scholars selected because of their engagement in a lifetime pursuit of knowledge and its dissemination. The faculty acquires a substantial role in actual decision making, though not on all subjects, because of its special competence in the various fields of learning. To enable it to carry out its responsibilities in learning and in teaching, the faculty is equipped with laboratories and libraries and provided with assistance from supporting staff.

Students are permitted to enter the university community as learners when they are judged qualified to use the educational opportunities offered by the institution, and they leave it after a period of study with certifications of various kinds as to their proficiency. Compared to the faculty and much of the staff, the students' stay within the university is relatively brief, but that stay should be as meaningful as the imagination and resources of the university can make it. The influence of students should therefore be less in the making of many decisions, although it is paramount in making some of them.

Members of what is called the university community have very dissimilar roles to play as members of that community. To respond to its basic objectives, the heightening of competence and knowledge, a university has to be not a people's democracy for all participants, but a hierarchically organized complex of estates in which decisions are made with the participation of those best qualified to make the particular decision, in the light not only of the internal structure of the university but of its external responsibilities to society at large. The one-man, one-vote referendum by faculty, staff, administration, and students simply does not apply reasonably to the complex business of university decision making.

In saying this, I am not saying that we could not improve our processes. We did have a problem of improving liaison among the organically separate parts, or estates, of the university, improving inputs to reach better decisions, and improving internal understanding of decisions. We had made much progress in recent years in developing better methods of interrelationships among administrators, faculty, and students.

Students in particular had been given greatly increased opportunities to voice their opinions through responsible channels on many more matters. Because of the need to review methods of government and to find further improvements, a Committee on University Governance had been formed whose membership included regents, administrators, faculty, and students. We needed more reasoned dialogue along these lines and fewer power plays and demands if we were to make actual progress toward better internal relations in the university community.

We had not met all the demands for power that had been advanced, frequently against one another, by different segments of the university. If the university were "reconstituted" as a political base for forays into the surrounding society, as some would have it, it would have ceased to be an effective place for the pursuit of learning and the development of high levels of competence. The university is founded on the proposition that some people know more than others. To convert it into an egalitarian democracy, with all votes equal, would be to repudiate the qualitative pursuit of learning.

In sum, I believe that our society is better served—and students are better served—if the University of Washington is permitted to stick to its purpose as an educational institution rather than a political instrument. Individuals, as students, should see the ultimate advantage to them in letting, and helping, the university function peaceably as an educational institution. The same individuals, as citizens concerned about various political issues of great moment, should use that much more aggressively the political channels available to them to persuade political representatives to follow the course of political action they desire.

Retirement
from the
University,
1973

BY THE FALL OF 1972 THE VIETNAM WAR WAS WINDING
down, and the peace treaty was to be signed in January 1973. Partly
because of this, campus unrest had subsided at the University of
Washington as well as at other universities across the country. It
seemed to me that a chapter was ending, both in the history of the
United States and in the history of the University of Washington.
Also by 1973, I was approaching the fifteenth year of my presidency.
For these reasons I decided that the time was nearing for me to step
down. Therefore in September 1972, I announced to the regents
that I felt I should retire from the presidency at the end of the academic year in 1973. I was further enabled to take this step because
of my confidence in the membership of the Board of Regents.

When I told the regents of my desire to retire, they sought to
persuade me to continue as president for several more years. However, my intention was firm and they ultimately accepted my decision but insisted that I should remain on campus even after I left
the presidency. To break the umbilical cord, my wife and I planned
to leave Seattle in the summer of 1973 for several months of travel

in the United States and Europe. When we returned to Seattle, we found that the regents had taken the initiative to procure an office for me in a very pleasant space in Miller Hall, which I have continued to occupy. My wife and I were also pleasantly surprised to find that the regents had given my name to the new Undergraduate Library.

Thus, by the time of my retirement from the presidency in June 1973, I had completed a pilgrimage of forty-five years through universities, starting with my entry into Dartmouth in 1928, and continuing through my years at Harvard, the University of Illinois, the University of Michigan, and the University of Washington — with brief digressions for service in the U.S. Navy and in the American Council of Learned Societies.

It is with some surprise that I have noted the twists and turns in my path to the present. A few years ago a newspaper reporter asked me to tell him about how I had planned my career to become a university president. I told him that I had not planned such a career objective, adding that I had become a university president in the same way that Britain had built its empire, in a long fit of absence of mind. The turns in the road were the results of initiatives on the part of others who approached me with job propositions that looked interesting. The only career decision I planned was to embark upon the extended educational course necessary to prepare myself to be a professor. The only time I started the process as an applicant for a job was at the conclusion of my doctorate at Harvard, when I became an instructor in history at the University of Illinois.

The job of education was never finished and each decade brought new problems. As a medievalist I learned of the struggle after the collapse of the Roman Empire to revive education in the monastic and cathedral schools, and of the invention of the universities. As a professor and academic administrator I have been a paticipant in the latest chapter about the universities and higher education. It continues to be for me a thrilling story about one of mankind's better inventions.

I close my account of pilgrimage through universities by returning once more to the words of Alfred North Whitehead. My
years of pilgrimage have convinced me that Whitehead was accurate when he defined the task of universities as "the creation of the
future, so far as rational thought and civilized modes of appreciation can affect the issue." He went on to say: "The future is big with
every possibility of achievement and of tragedy."

The creation of the future seems today, even more than when
Whitehead wrote those words, to describe the irreplaceable responsibility still confronting universities.

Postscript:
A New Career in
Medical Education
by Keith Benson

FOLLOWING HIS RETIREMENT AND HIS SUMMER OF travel, President Odegaard returned to Seattle in 1973 to work on what became essentially a new career, medical education. In a sense, this was a logical outgrowth of his relationship with one of his former faculty colleagues, Professor Charles Bodemer. Bodemer, an anatomist by training but one who also became a noted historian of biology (embryology) and medicine, was able to convince Odegaard and the School of Medicine to establish a Department of Biomedical History within the medical school. Bodemer's plan, which Odegaard enthusiastically embraced in 1966, was to develop a humanities department as an antidote to the growing specialization of medicine, which increasingly emphasized the scientific aspects of medicine often to the detriment of the humanistic aspects of the field. Bodemer, to whom Odegaard referred as a "rare bird" because of his broad interests, opened the new department in 1968 with promises from his president that he would do anything to encourage the expansion of the program.

Odegaard's concern about the direction of medical education

was one that was not restricted to medicine, but was aimed at the type of education in the sciences that typified research universities. As early as 1965, he astonished a National Academy of Sciences meeting in Seattle by saying that "scientism" had invaded too many universities, often aided by "the contemptuous attitude of some scientists toward moral problems." As he told his faculty during his annual report of that year, it was the duty of university faculty to address moral issues and to teach values, not just to address the facts of science. Thus, Bodemer was encouraged to expand the new department toward ethical issues in medicine, an expansion he accomplished by hiring Thomas McCormick on a part-time basis to discuss issues of death and dying with the medical students.

Odegaard had become intensely interested in the problems facing an increasingly scientific medicine fairly early in his administrative career. He had agreed to serve on the Millis Commission, which was formally known as the Citizens Commission on Graduate education of the American Medical Association, from 1963 to 1966. During this time, the commission studied the impact of the change in American medicine as it began to increasingly emphasize the development of medical specialties at the expense of general practice. This service was quickly followed by tenures on five additional national commissions related to medical affairs, including the National Advisory Health Council (1964–68), the National Commission on Health Manpower (1966–67), and the Board of Directors of the Clinical Scholars Program of the Robert Wood Johnson Foundation (1978 for federal medical research dollars. Additionally, his reputation as an astute observer of medical education and health service was reinforced when he was asked by Clark Kerr, chairman of the Carnegie Council on Policy Studies in Higher Education, to evaluate the success of the federal government's Area Health Education Center contracts with eleven universities, located in parts of the United States in which the health care delivery system often involved joining partnerships between the medical school in that particular region and area health education centers located at some distance from the medical school. The original report he wrote, *Area Health Education Centers: The Pioneering Years, 1972–1978,* was followed by a detailed discussion of each of his observations on the eleven sites and appeared two years later (1980) as *Eleven Area Health Education Centers: The View from the Grass Roots.* In both reports, it is clear that what impressed Odegaard most was the need for the physicians in training to complement their training in the science of medicine with a keen sense of the importance of considering the patient as an individual. And the latter consideration was one that emphasized the role of values, morals, and ethics, all of which were often missing from the modern medical school curriculum.

Increasingly, Odegaard became a critic and skeptic of the modern scientific mode of training physicians, a model he often deplored as the "biomedical model" to the exclusion of any attention to the physician-patient relationship. The essential issue was the disappearance of the concern for the patient as medical schools rushed to become competitive research centers. Receiving support from the Henry J. Kaiser Family Foundation, he then directed his attention to provide his own reflections on the state of American medical education. His book, *Dear Doctor: A Personal Letter to a Physician,* was published in 1986.

Dr. Paul Beeson, a faculty colleague of Odegaard's at the University of Washington, wrote the foreword to the book, a foreword that provided a clear overview of Odegaard's concerns: "No one can deny, then, that the world of medicine is passing through an uncomfortable and troubling period, or that it has need for wise counsel such as we are given in 'Dear Doctor.' I can attest that the document has been a powerful educational instrument for me, as I think it will be for others. . . . Odegaard helps us to see ourselves and the society we belong to, and argues that we should aim to achieve a better balance in our modern scientist-healers, a balance that is appropriate to the physician's role in society."

Then, illustrating that his skills as an historian had not diminished as a result of the years he spent as an university administrator, Odegaard addressed himself to his reader, his "Dear Doctor," by presenting a brief historical overview of American medicine. In this remarkable overview, he clearly illustrated the rise of science in American medicine as science emerged as one of the major characteristics of the modern research university. Unfortunately, the attention to biomedical explanations of disease, which had resulted in unprecedented knowledge about and control over disease, was done at the cost of attention to the patient as a diseased entity. And while he noted that C. P. Snow wrote about the developing "Two Cultures" phenomenon in the modern university, it was the culture of science that emerged triumphant to lead American medicine at the end of the twentieth century.

Yet, Odegaard claimed, there were signs of internal criticism and reflection. The 1984 report of the Panel on the General Professional Education of the Physician and College Preparation for Medicine (GPEP report of the Association of American Medical Colleges) made a strong argument to redirect medical practitioners back to the concerns of their patients: "This general conclusion calls for a shift in emphasis among the skills, values, and attitudes taught in medical school: a limitation in the volume of factual information medical students are expected to commit to memory; a better enunciation of the levels of knowledge and skills required at each step in medical education; changes in educational settings; and an emphasis on the responsibility of physicians to patients and communities."

This report was followed by commentary from the American Association of Medical Colleges stating the following: "The working group recommends that faculties integrate into the common curriculum materials that will provide students with a working knowledge of the ethical dimensions and social context of medicine in addition to an understanding of biological principles and their application to patient care."

Yet, despite these clear recommendations for changes in the curriculum, the hold of the biomedical model was too strong. Facing an increasingly technologically based medicine, most American medical schools retained their emphasis on the biomedical model.

Odegaard continued to work within his own institution for change, however. Encouraged by physicians, such as Paul Beeson, Thomas Inui, and Theodore Phillips, he pressed his concerns to whatever audience would listen. In 1988, he served as one of the most eloquent spokespersons to hire Professor Albert Jonsen, one of the country's leading medical ethicists, to head the Department of Biomedical History, which had been without a chair following the untimely death of Professor Bodemer in 1986. Almost immediately, the new emphasis of the department, again encouraged by Odegaard, became apparent when it was renamed the Department of Medical History *and Ethics*. Finally, and over fifteen years after he left the presidency, Odegaard had made a significant inroad into what he considered to be the required mission of the University of Washington, especially in its School of Medicine. That is, now it overtly recognized the role of values and ethics in the education of new physicians.

But the changes at the University of Washington did not satisfy Odegaard. Noting, correctly, that medical education still resisted attention to the patient-physician relationship, Odegaard continued to emphasize his interests toward humanizing medicine well into the 1990s. More needed to be done to expose young physicians to the "other culture" of medicine: "I claim only that the process of education for the physician's role has not provided sufficient instruction on the human relationship between the patient and the physician. Despite this deficiency there are cases—and I have seen some myself—that embody evidence of a physician's careful listening and of unusual awareness of and sensitivity to the patient's feelings. But not enough opportunity has been provided in medical education to help all future physicians acquire the relevant knowledge and skill to become good listeners."

It may seem remarkable that this extremely accomplished medieval historian, Navy officer, educational leader, and university administrator should have made such a profound contribution to American medical education. After all, he was not a physician, nor had he served in any capacity as a medical school administrator prior to his retirement years. But perhaps Odegaard had been conditioned by his own experiences in witnessing the illness and death of his beloved wife. While the treatment she received was of the highest scientific nature, he always felt it lacked a human dimension. But even more importantly, his concern about medical education mirrored Odegaard's lifelong interest in communication. His administrative structure at the University of Washington was one that was constructed to make communication more effective. When he sought to involve the faculty within the University administration more effectively, again he emphasized communication channels. As he saw the University compete within the state for access to higher education's limited funds, again he sought to develop modes of communication within the state's higher education community. Finally, when the University exploded under the pressure of American society's increasing problems surrounding race, sex, environment, and international affairs, his response was to increase the opportunities to communicate.

For Odegaard, medicine represented the most fundamental of communication channels. After all, the most intimate relationship in modern society, save that of the family, is the relationship of the patient and physician. As the emphasis upon science increased in American society generally, it acted to remove the human dimension of medicine. As this trend was first witnessed by the rise of the biomedical model in the early twentieth century, then brought forcibly "home" with the demise of the general practitioner, patients of the American medical system found themselves treated too often as entities, with little or no attention to their sense of personal identity.

"Enlightenment has to take place in the minds of people," he wrote. "I have always argued for the broader awareness of responsible patterns of behavior. We are making progress, but cultural development is a long struggle."